"So long as there are earnest believers in the world, they will always wish to punish opinions, even if their judgment tells them it is unwise and their conscience that it is wrong." – Walter Bagehot

Appeal to Pragmatism

This collection of essays evolved over a year long period of rural living which left me much time for contemplation and rumination. I had the great luxury of time, time to read in a serious way and be engrossed in politics and political discussions. These essays were born out of a larger question of why to advocate certain political ideas, why being the operative word. Throughout time spent on reading, watching, discussing, and contemplating, a common theme started to emerge. I believe that American politics and political discussions have become too ideological, that is our cognition has become centered on ideology. Our elected public servants[1] and our political discussions have become beholden to ideology, it has poisoned our ability to think critically about issues and problems. We no longer seek to find the most effective solution to our problems, but to find the solution that fits our predisposed ideology. In short we have lost our ability to objectively analysis problems, to compromise, and be pragmatic in our solutions. United States elected public servants, political commentators, and each citizen would gain much by adopting more objective, pragmatic ways of thinking and analyzing problems. I believe the United States will be able to craft better policies and solutions to the myriad of problems it is currently confronting be adopting a more pragmatic approach to policy making. This collection of essays is an appeal to pragmatism for the United States.

A significant downside to a lack of pragmatic thinking in the United States is that it produces policy solutions that do not have the best interests of the United States at heart. We are not asking the question, "What is the most effective policy for the United States?" but rather, "What is the most effective policy for the United States that fits my preexisting political ideology?" This method of thinking prioritizes political ideology over the most effective solution to the problem in question. The desire of finding a solution within or that conforms to a political ideology overshadows the desire of finding the most effective solution for the United States. Prioritizing political ideology causes our elected public servants to limit the spectrum of their possible solutions, usually to either left or right ideology. It eliminates the possibility of a hybrid solution to a problem that employs both left and right ideology. The elected public servants of the United States need to be less beholden to ideology and more pragmatic in crafting solution to our problems.

In addition to our elected officials crafting pragmatic solutions to problems, we need political commentary and general public debate[2] to be less beholden to ideology and think more pragmatically. Being so beholden to political ideology has rendered public debate in the United States virtually nonexistent. Non-eristic debate is about the process of discovering or uncovering

---

[1] I use the term elected public servant deliberately, instead of politician.

[2] I mention general public debate, because political debate does not just occur on televised 'debates' or in Congress. The vast majority of debate in the United States happens in coffee houses, dinner tables, parties and other public/private forms every day. These debates are just as important as any televised debate on CSPAN.

a truth. The end goal of non-eristic debate is truth. Our public debates in the United States have become too eristic; they are about proving a point or persuading others to one's argument. For example, presidential debates are more about candidates being perceived a certain way and outlining why a particular political position is better than their opponents. A presidential debate about healthcare is not about determining the most effective solution that provides the most efficient healthcare system for the needs of the United States; it is about convincing viewers that their plans are the most effective. Ideology being more influential than pragmatic thinking exacerbates the decline and the greatest inhibitor of non-eristic debate. How can we try to find the most effective solution for a problem if we are unable to consider any solutions or aspects outside our particular political ideology?

The most pragmatic elected public servants in the United States are mayors. Mayors are the most pragmatic because they are closer to problems and their solutions to those problems than any other elected public servants. Mayors are also the easiest to connect to their solutions to problems and thus, the easiest to hold accountable for the results of their solutions. Mayors do not have the luxury of hiding behind vague existential threats like terrorism, communism, the religious right, the left wing agenda, or the right wing agenda as national politicians can. Mayors are forced to find pragmatic solutions to problems that are the most effective because they are held to a greater degree of accountability. They cannot blame their failures on others as easily or distract their constituents by evoking vague existential threats. Mayors are often the most willing to adopt creative solutions to problems and work with opposing political parties. Cory Booker, the former mayor of Newark, NJ is a prominent example of a pragmatic elected public servant. Mayor Booker negotiated public sector cutbacks with unions, expanded government resources for those seeking work, and embraced public-private partnerships. The incredible results in Newark during his tenure are sufficient evidence. I think we should consider mayors as a more viable option in nationwide elections; their experience is more suited to pragmatic thinking. Cities have become the true engines of policy innovation in the United States by embracing more objective pragmatic thinking. We also need to hold our national elected officials more accountable as well.

In an ideal situation, an elected public servant would be able to eliminate a government program simply because by objective measures it does not work. As time elapses, original factors governing problems and their solutions change. Economic conditions, demographics, and society change with time. It is often the case that conditions outgrow a problem or outgrow the original solution to that problem rendering the solution and perhaps the problem irrelevant. It would be nice if our elected public servants could eliminate a government program for those reasons. Or perhaps, several academic studies have been conducted and they come to the conclusion, in an objective analysis, that the government program in question is ineffectual. The pragmatic solution would be to eliminate the program. Unfortunately, in our current world where ideology holds so much sway over our thinking, we cannot get rid of that government program. That government program becomes more than just that specific program. It becomes a representation of whether particular political ideologies are possible. The right declares the death of government programs and how government policies are ineffectual and, as is often the case with the right, immoral. The left holds up the program as a defense of government's ability to help individuals and the role the government plays in solving problems in the economy and society. In reality the operative question is the effectiveness of the government program in question, not whether government can work to solve problems or not. I think it would be substantially more productive for the United States to view programs and solutions in this way, not as part of a larger ideology. I would implore United States elected public servants to move towards a more objective, pragmatic, fact driven government.

List of Essays

Dedicated to Walter Bagehot

Disclaimer

As with anything written and then put forth into the public space, the essays that appear in this book will no doubt receive a variety of reactions. I welcome all reactions and any discussions, if any at all were to occur. In order to perhaps defray any confusion or perceived intent, I will briefly state my intentions and motivations for writing this collection of essays.

I don't have any pretenses of changing the way the American people analyze and think about political issues with this book. I simply wish to add a small bit that hopefully may make a few individuals pause for a brief moment and think about the state of the American electorate and how we think.

The essays that follow are more of a thought exercise, a series of hypothetical postulations, than a serious academic work. I have not used proper academic reference citations, it citations are used at all. Academic resources have been used in writing each essay, but are not the main point of each essay. If one is looking for an academic book, one will not find it in the proceeding pages. This collection of essays is meant for others to think about current political, social, and economic problems, and less about the possible solutions I highlight. Facts and figures are less important than the thought process utilized, which is the most important aspect of an argument. It is with this aim in mind I ask the reader to proceed.

Finally, the ideas contained within these essays are not a definitive representation of my ideas. They are merely a snapshot of how I was thinking at the time they were written. I hope to keep thinking and progressing with my thoughts in the future. If the past is a reliable indicator, I will no doubt change my mind many times on these issues over the course of the coming years.

I hope you enjoy.

"The best reason why Monarchy is a strong government is, that it is an intelligible government. The mass of mankind understand it, and they hardly anywhere in the world understand any other." – Walter Bagehot

Immigration Reform

Current United States immigration policy must address two primary areas of concern; one area of long-term structural importance to United States immigration policy and the other area of a stand-alone, one off incident that achieves most attention and news coverage.

The first immigration policy area of concern that is of long-term structural importance to the United States deals with the kind of immigrants our system attracts and allows to immigrate. Our current immigration policy does not place enough emphasis on attracting and retaining educated and highly skilled immigrants and foreign students studying in the United States. The current policy's lack of ability to attract and retain educated and skilled immigrants places the United States at a competitive disadvantage in comparison to other developed countries with more progressive immigration systems such as Canada and Australia. Even if the United States is able to educate its own citizens to meet the requirements of a more technology based economy, which it is not currently doing, the results from education will take ten years or more to manifest. The United States needs educated and skilled immigrants for the economy to thrive in the short and intermediate terms until gains in our education system can take effect.

The second immigration policy area of concern is dealing with the approximately 12 million people who have entered and now reside in the United States illegally. While these 12 million people are a side issue to long-term structural immigration policy reform, their situation has captivated and occupied the lion share of media coverage on any immigration debate and become the all-encompassing center of any proposed immigration debate in the United States federal government. Without addressing the issues of the 12 million people illegally residing in the United States, enacting long-term structural reform that will allow the United States to compete internationally for the workers its economy needs will not be possible. The United States must provide a solution that brings these 12 million illegal residents out of the shadows, allows them to contribute to the mainstream economy, and address the cause of the massive 12 million illegal resident problems.

With all of the considerations discussed in the previous paragraph, I advocate a two pronged immigration reform policy. The first prong is aimed at long-term structural change to the United States immigration system in order to attract more educated and highly skilled immigrants from around the world. The second prong is to bring the current 12 million illegal residents out of the shadows, contributing to the United States economy, and to provide a solution to the cause of the phenomena that allowed them to enter and reside illegally in the United States.

In order to attract educated and highly skilled immigrants to the United States I advocate that the United States place a clear emphasis on these immigrants in our immigration system and make our policies more like those of Canada and Australia who are attracting more educated and highly skilled immigrants per capita than the United States. The American economy has changed greatly from the late 1800s to our present time, the type of jobs our economy requires have changed along with our economy. The United States economy in decades past had a much greater capacity to absorb and provide jobs for uneducated and unskilled immigrants, currently the United States economy has a relatively lower ability to absorb and provide jobs for uneducated and unskilled immigrants, our immigration system and policy should reflect these changes in economic conditions. And finally, I advocate a policy that legalizes all of the 12 million illegal residents without a criminal record currently in the United States as legal guest workers and provides those who wish with the option of a path to citizenship, those who choose not to become citizens may remain as legal guest workers. A path to citizenship for the 12 million illegal residents in the United States will not be a broader policy initiative; it will be a one off policy that applies specifically to the 12 million illegals currently residing in the United States and will not be extended to future individuals who illegally gain entry and reside in the United States.

The United States was founded by immigrants from Europe and enriched throughout the ensuing years by immigrants from every corner of the world.[3] The United States for much of its history had a largely agrarian economy which was bolstered and enabled by large areas of cheap or free land for internal migrants and immigrants to cultivate.[4] Americans expanded westward at an incredible rate. Farming and farm work at that time were types of work that did not require a formal education or highly trained skills. Many immigrants had been farmers or farm laborers in their countries of origin, continuing their profession in North American with perhaps more and higher quality land. Farming also is a profession in which language skills were not of paramount importance given that farms tend to be more isolated and the work requires minimal collaboration compared to other professions at the time. A lawyer or salesperson for example must effectively communicate their ideas and what they are selling to the native speaking population, compared to a farmer who mostly toils alone with their family on an isolated plot of land. Given the availability of land, low education and skill requirements for entry, and lack of language requirements, agriculture was a very attractive profession for many immigrants to the United States. Given that from the creation of the United States up to the industrial revolution in the late 1800s the majority of the American economy was employed in agriculture, the United States had a very large capacity to absorb large numbers of uneducated and/or unskilled immigrants, being able to provide suitable jobs on which to live on for immigrants.

---

[3] This statement is not claiming that people did not live and prosper within the geographic limits of the current United States. Native Americans were the first inhabits of North America. The United States was derived at its formation on the model of a European nation state. The original 13 colonies were modeled as extensions of European nation states. It is solely in reference to origins of the United States under the modern nation state model that predominates the world today and has for the at the very least the past 300 years.

[4] Again it should be noted that a portion of this land was already occupied by Native Americans. Given the policies and views toward of the federal government and general population at the time to the legality of Native American claims to land, one can consider the vast majority of 'unsettled' land open for internal migrants and immigrants.

The industrial revolution transformed the American economy, adding new kinds of jobs for uneducated and/or unskilled immigrants. Millions were able to find work in factories within the metropolitan areas of cities. Factory jobs provided similar opportunities that farming occupations had previously in American history. The vast majority of factory jobs required no education and very little if any specific skills. Performing a specific repetitive task over and over again also comes with few language barriers to entry. Factory jobs were jobs that not only uneducated, unskilled internal migrants from farms could perform but also uneducated, unskilled immigrants without significant command of the English language could perform as well. The industrial revolution provided millions of immigrants with occupations in the United States; from Italians to Germans to Eastern Europeans to Chinese to many other types of immigrants. While urban conditions in immigrant areas would be considered by today's standards beyond deplorable, the American economy was able to provide suitable jobs for uneducated and unskilled immigrants in sufficient quantities for the United States to absorb large numbers of uneducated and/or unskilled immigrants.

In 1950, the economic sector break down of employment in the United States incorporated both agriculture and manufacturing in large proportions, the United States still had the economic capacity to absorb large numbers of uneducated and/or unskilled immigrants. In 1950 approximately 25% of workers were employed in agriculture and 45% were employed in manufacturing, make a 70% share of Americans employed in either agriculture or manufacturing. While land had been mostly claimed and utilized, the agricultural industry could still offer large numbers of labor jobs that required very little if any formal education, skills, or English language skills. The overwhelming number of those employed in manufacturing were employed as workers, occupations that still had very few barriers to entry from education, skills, and language. Given that 70% of the American economy revolved around agriculture and manufacturing the United States in the 1950s had the ability to absorb large numbers of uneducated and/or unskilled immigrants.

Currently agriculture represents between 2% and 3% of the American workforce and manufacturing represents 16% of the workforce. Combined agriculture and manufacturing, the traditional areas of employment for uneducated and/or unskilled immigrants without English language skills, represent at most, rounded up 20% of the American workforce. This is a 50% drop in share of the workforce from 1950 for agriculture and manufacturing. Compared to past economic conditions in American history, agriculture and manufacturing are not industries able to absorb large numbers of immigrants. With the increased mechanization of the agricultural industry, fewer uneducated and/or unskilled workers are needed, and the workers that the agricultural industry does need are educated workers who can operate increasing complex and computerized machines. Employment in the manufacturing industry is little different from the agricultural industry. After decades of outsourcing which saw the manufacturing share of jobs in the US economy shrink drastically, manufacturing jobs are starting to return to the United States, but they are not the manufacturing jobs of previous eras. Manufacturing is becoming increasing more automated and computerized. These new manufacturing jobs require those with education and specific skills to operate more automated and computerized manufacturing equipment and factories. An example of the increased automation and computerization of American factories lies with Nike. Nike has moved some production of shoes from Vietnam to the United States. They have not moved to the United States because American labor cost have gone down or because Vietnamese labor costs have risen sharply, they are moving production back to the United States because Nike has developed a machine that can produce the main components of a single show on its own. Their new machine can perform the jobs that many workers use to perform and without fatigue and greater uniformity. Nike needs educated workers to operate their new, more complex machine, which is a significant capital expense. What one gleams from the agricultural and manufacturing employment data is that the agricultural and manufacturing sectors are no longer large enough to provide suitable jobs for large numbers of uneducated and/or unskilled immigrants.

Today the United States economy is comprised much less of agricultural and manufacturing jobs. Jobs and occupations in service industries now employ the majority of Americans. Service sector jobs require a greater knowledge of the English language and general English proficiency. Unlike agricultural and manufacturing jobs in past American economic eras, service sector jobs have a language barrier to entry.

When one considers the fact that the agricultural and manufacturing sectors comprise a substantially smaller portion of the American workforce, two areas which have historically been the largest providers of jobs to uneducated and/or unskilled immigrants, and the substantial growth of service sector jobs, with their increased language barriers, as a proportion of the American workforce, one irrevocably comes to the conclusion that the United States in 2014 does not have the same capacity to absorb large numbers of uneducated and/or unskilled immigrants lacking English skills as it did in previous eras of large scale immigration. If immigrants want to find jobs that can support themselves and possible their families, they will need to have knowledge of the English language and be much more educated or skilled than immigrants in the past. Many politicians who make comparisons to the economic potential of immigrants in past eras of immigration to the United States are often making false comparisons with eras of different economic realities for immigrants. The United States lack of economic capacity to absorb large numbers of uneducated and/or unskilled immigrants without language skills should be a primary and very powerful motivator towards adopting an immigration system and policies that favor higher proportions of educated and skilled immigrants with knowledge of the English language. Our immigration system and policies should reflect our economic capacity to provide jobs for incoming immigrants.

Canada and Australia have changed their immigration systems to primarily attract and take in a large proportion of educated and highly skilled immigrants with knowledge of English. These types of immigrants are the most likely to be financially successful in their new countries and by most measures are much better integrated into their receiving societies than other immigrants. Their financial success means they are substantially less likely to utilize public assistance programs and the overwhelming vast majority contributes more money in taxes than they consume in government benefits and programs. Compared to other types of immigrants, the educated and highly skilled immigrants are a much better value proposition for the destination country. Educated and highly skilled immigrants are also more likely to hold liberal and tolerant western views on such topics as women's rights, religions freedom and the right to offend, freedom of speech, tolerance for other races, and other western values. Given that they contribute more than they receive from the government and that they are better integrated into societies and culture of their destination countries, educated and skilled immigrants provide a better value to western countries.

Currently there is a mismatch in employment in the United States. Employers are unable to find employees who meet the qualifications for jobs being offered. In fewer places is this mismatch illustrated in starker contrast than in Silicon Valley. Silicon Valley, the birthplace and center of the technology industry, is unable to find the quantities of programmers and engineers they require. Many prominent Silicon Valley executives, such as Facebook's Mark Zuckerberg, have personally lobbied the Obama administration to advocate for immigration reform to allow them to hire more qualified programmers and computer engineers as well as making it easier for foreign students studying in the United States to come, stay, and work in the United States. The tech industry in Silicon Valley needs adequate numbers of qualified workers to continue growing and maintain its position as the leading technology center in the world. Immigration reform is needed to give Silicon Valley the workers it needs.

The United States needs reform to the structure of our immigration system. If the United States wishes to remain competitive in the world, it must prioritize educated and highly skilled immigrants and admit more educated and highly skilled immigrants than uneducated immigrants without skills. I propose the United States adopt immigration policies similar to those of Canada and Australia in order to augment the United States economy.

The second prong that I have proposed requires finding a solution that allows the 12 million illegal residents in the United States to come out of the shadows and contribute to the American economy and provides a solution for the cause the illegal entrant phenomena, while giving the 12 million illegal residents as many options as possible.

One must start with the fact that the 12 million illegal residents have gained entry to the United States and barring an extreme outlier event, they are here to stay. Physically and forcefully removing the entire 12 million people who have illegally gained entry into the United States would be an expensive and draconian process that would not be optimal economically or morally pleasing. Currently there are no serious[5] proposals in the federal government that involve physically removing and deporting 12 million people. It would seem that the American

---

[5] Placing a large emphasis on the word 'serious'

people and their elected officials do not wish to separate families and remove members of communities in mass and thus have rejected the idea of mass deportations. The United States is then left at an impasse; continue with the status quo which involves 12 million people not fully contributing to the United States economy and living lives in the shadows or providing a way to legalize their status in the United States thus allowing them to contribute more fully to the United States economy. The economic benefits of legalizing the 12 million illegal residents in the United States far exceed the economic benefits in our current status quo. Without question a legalized status for the 12 million illegal residents is vastly preferable to the current status quo, considering that these 12 million people will remain in the United States whether legalized or not.

I advocate for a multiple tiered program that legalizes all 12 million illegal residents without criminal records to work and live in the United States, provides a path to United States citizenship for those illegal residents who wish to become citizens, and provides some degree of alleviation for the cause of the illegal resident phenomena so that it can be diminished or wholly avoided in the future.

The first tier should be the legalization of the 12 million illegal residents without a criminal record. I advocate creating a one year registration period, during which those illegally residing in the United States may register with the United States government and if found to not possess a criminal record, will be granted guest worker status in the United States. Guest worker status will not entail the recipient to American citizenship, but will allow the recipient to legally work and live in the United States. A guest worker may travel back and forth to their country of origin freely to visit family and make use of the legal banking system to transfer money. The will pay United States taxes on income earned in the United States and have the same access to public services as legal residents. Legalizing the 12 million illegal residents who do not possess criminal records will allow them to more fully contribute to the United States economy and will be economically beneficial for the United States. At the end of the designated one year registration period, any illegal resident who has failed to register with the United States government or has a criminal record will lose the ability to become a guest worker and if discovered will be deported. Currently the United States has a policy of not pursuing illegal residents past the border[6] and not pursuing illegal migrants who are living illegal in the United States. After the one year registration period has expired, the policy of United States border and law enforcement will change. Law enforcement will aggressively pursue illegal migrants past the border conduct investigations into illegal residents who are living in communities throughout the United States. If discovered these illegal residents will be deported to their country of origin. The above described policies will be enacted in order to deter future individuals who seek to gain

---

[6] The 12 million people illegally residing in the United States come from a wide range of origin countries from around the world. But we must recognize that the overwhelming vast majority of illegal residents in the United States originate from Mexico and Central America. Any resolution to the current 12 million illegal resident problem in the United States must take this previously mentioned fact into account. If in the course of this essay I insinuate or associate illegal residents with Mexico and Central America, it is only in recognition of the majority.

entry illegally to the United States. These harsh laws are designed to demonstrate that the guest worker status conferred on the current 12 million illegal residents without criminal records is a one-time provision that will not be extended to future illegal residents.

Giving those of the 12 million illegal residents who do not have a criminal record guest worker status should be part of a larger initiative to reinstate a general guest worker program with Mexico and Central American countries. Lack of economic growth and general economic stagnation in Mexico coupled with strong economic growth in the United States created significant push and pull factors for mass scale Mexican immigration into the United States from the 1990s to the 2007 financial crisis. The quantity of Mexicans demanding entry to work in the United States far exceeded the quantity of immigrants the United States was willing to accommodate which created an imbalance which lead many Mexicans who could not enter the United States legally to gain entry illegally. The economic recession following the 2007 financial crisis combined with stronger economic growth in Mexico has very much eliminated the previous push and pull factors for Mexicans to seek illegal entry into the United States. Many studies actually show a decrease in the illegal resident population in the United States as many Mexicans choose to return home to Mexico. While the conditions that created the current 12 million illegal resident phenomena in the United States have abated, it is not unreasonable that they may come into being and persist again in the future. The United States needs to provide a workable solution to prevent another phenomenon of mass numbers of illegal residents.

I propose the United States reinstall a guest worker program to provide a legal avenue for Mexicans and Central Americans seeking to enter the United States to work but who do not wish to become citizens. A legal guest worker system will provide a constructive way for the United States to channel the forces causing Mexicans and Central Americans to gain entry to the United States legally or illegally. A legal guest worker system will give the United States a degree of control over the phenomena of illegal migration by giving would be migrants a legal outlet which the United States retains control over. A legal guest worker program can also bring economic benefits for the United States economy without the cost of providing services to citizens. It will allow United States employers to access a ready pool of labor for which they need and American citizens are not able to fill. The United States government will also gain tax revenue from the work performed by guest workers. Several countries around the world have utilized guest worker programs successfully, a prime example being Germany. The German guest worker program has been incredible successful in the filling the labor shortages brought about by decreasing German fertility rates. Giving Mexicans and Central Americans who want to work in the United States guest worker status instead of citizenship also fits into larger immigration reform aimed at reorienting the United States immigration system towards educated and highly skilled immigrants. The average Mexican and Central American immigrant is uneducated and unskilled by Mexican and Central American standards, let alone American standards. The average Mexican and Central American immigrant also poses little if any practical knowledge of the English language. Compared to substantially more qualified immigrants from other geographic and socio-economic areas who are much more educated, skilled, and possess knowledge of English, Mexican and Central American immigrants are undesirable for the American economy of the present and future. A guest worker program allows the United States to utilize workers for a the economic needs they are needed for, provide a legal outlet for the pressures encouraging millions of people to seek illegal entry and residence in the United States, as well as complementing an immigration system which seeks to attract educated and highly skilled immigrants with knowledge of English.

After legalizing those of the current 12 million illegal residents without a criminal record as guest workers, the United States should then provide those who wish, the option of entering into a process that would lead, those who choose to participate, to American citizenship. After the yearlong registration period has ended and those of the 12 million illegal residents without a criminal record who wanted to register have registered and been awarded guest worker status, another yearlong registration period should be allowed for those with newly granted guest worker status who wish to enter into a process of becoming an American citizen. As of the time of this writing, members of the Republican and Democratic parties in Congress had agreed on a 13 year time span[7] for a process of obtaining American citizenship for the 12 million illegal immigrants. Therefore, I propose a 13 year process, for those of the 12 million illegal residents who are granted guest worker status, to become American citizens. This process towards American citizenship will be entirely optional and each individual will have a year after being granted guest worker status to decide. If they wish to remain guest workers and legally work in the United States they may retain that guest worker status for the rest of their lives. Perhaps many who choose guest worker status believe this course the best economically or have a patriotic passion for their country of origin. Whatever their reason, the decision to become an American citizen is entirely their decision. After the one year registration period for the American citizenship process has expired, those who choose guest worker status will not be able to reenroll and will not have the option of becoming American citizens. For those who choose the 13 year process to become American citizens, there will be no option of holding dual citizenship. Becoming an American citizen through this special citizenship process requires the successful participants to renounce the citizenship of their country of origin and all the rights that country's citizenship entails. Whether one chooses to remain a guest worker or chooses the path towards United States citizenship, all of the 12 million illegal residents without criminal records will be legalized, brought out of the shadows, and contribute fully to the United States economy.

If the United States adopts the course of action described above for the 12 million illegal residents in the United States, the United States will be able to most effectively resolve the unique political situation of the 12 million illegal residents, enabling the United States to address

---

[7] In my opinion, 13 years is a bit long, but given that both relevant political parties have agreed on this number and how rare agreement between these parties has become these days, I will use it for the sake of efficiency.

long-term immigration reform. By providing the 12 million illegal residents without criminal records the option between being a legal guest worker and becoming an American citizen, the United States is allowing the 12 million illegal residents to choose their outcome. While many elected public servants may disagree with and oppose allowing some of the 12 million illegal residents to become legal guest workers instead of citizens or become citizens instead of guest workers, at the end of the day I believe it best to give those directly affected more options to decide their fate and how they wish to live their lives.

As a final note on the proposed solutions to the 12 million illegal residents in the United States, increased spending on border security and on law enforcements ability to locate and arrest those who gain illegal entry and illegally reside in the United States will have to accompany these proposals in order to appease certain right wing elements in the United States Congress. While a waste of the United States' scarce resources, however increased funding for border security and law enforcement is a political necessity that must accompany the other proposes in order to enact them. This small inconvenience and waste is worth the benefits of the overall package.

Education

The United States education system presents a myriad of problems in enacting system wide reform, primarily stemming from extreme decentralization and localization as well as being funded by a variety of different methods. Given these challenges to reform, I will divide any advocacy for education reform programs into two distinct groups; those relating to kindergarten through high school education and those relating to university education. Given the extreme localization of our education system, I will further divide responsibilities and capacity for reasonable reform measures between local governments, state governments, federal governments, and combinations of the three governments. Within these guises I will propose a few measures and general policy focuses to improve the quality of education for children and young adults in the United States. I will argue for a new generation of land grant colleges specializing in computer science and technology to provide affordable university education in areas of current and future American economic need. Next I will argue for a new orientation of education programs with a primary aim of intertwining families in the education process from the earliest age of students. Finally I will argue for the federal government to withhold funding for a variety of projects to states until the states force local communities, which provide most individual school funding, to raise more revenue for their local school systems themselves.[8] In return the federal government will provide more funding to states and thus to local communities for schools which will partially aide in the increase of revenue from each localities citizens. If these steps prescribed are enacted I believe we can increase the education and thus the capacities of the American workforce to not only endure, but thrive in the globally competitive world.

In the late 1800's the United States was on the cusp of its industrial revolution, a technological and economic movement that would transform the United States into the world's largest and most dynamic economy. Railroads and telegraph lines were crisscrossing the nation. Americans were utilizing and exploiting many new technologies. The United States needed a new class of engineers, architects, and workers to master and maximize these new technologies. During this era the United States began expanding and really utilizing a system of land grant universities to produce the engineers of the future. Universities such as Cornell, Ohio State, and many others were started on public land with aide from public funds to provide affordable education to the public and to train the workforce in the demands of new technology. These engineers, who were educated at these intuitions, designed and created railroads, skyscrapers, automobiles, planes, and seemingly countless products and devices which substantially bettered the quality of life of Americans. With the invention and widespread adoption of the internet, the next revolution has been and is sweeping across not just the United States but the world. The

---

[8] I realize how series and draconian this last propose seems. I also realize how political unfeasible this may seem as well. However I believe it is the most effective and the only way to achieve nationwide long-term systemic change to the education system. It will require our elected public servants to exercise no small degree of political capital and stomach no small degree of negative public sentiment.

technology revolution is changing the way people shop, interact, and work, in short it is radically changing the world. The United States needs to adapt and change to the new demands and opportunities of the technology revolutionized world. We need to change our education system to adapt to the new requirements of the technology revolution.

A simple, time tested way of augmenting our system for the technology revolution is to create a series of land grant universities for computer science and technology to train the next generation of engineers for the technology and jobs of our new technological and economic era, a public land grant Massachusetts Institute of Technology in every state. Public universities have traditionally been the best avenue for advancement into the middle class for Americans. We need to help our public universities continue to provide an avenue for Americans into the middle class by giving Americans public universities that educate them for in demand jobs of the future. The United States has created a hot bed of technological innovation in Silicon Valley. The United States needs to provide firms in Silicon Valley with highly trained workers to aide in the incredible innovation and products being produced there. Public universities focused on computer science and technology can provide education for future jobs to large numbers of Americans at affordable prices. Creating a capable workforce with the skills for the technology revolution is paramount to economic success of the American people domestically, but is also incredibly necessary in a globally competitive world where the United States does not have a monopoly on technological innovation and firms can easily outsource jobs to workers in other countries. Given current levels of economic competition from other countries never experienced before by previous generations of Americans, creating a workforce with the knowledge and skills needed to compete in the global economy is paramount as well. Americans are no longer competing only with themselves. While the United States is currently the world's largest economy, we cannot rest on our laurels.

In order to achieve a drastic increase in public land grant universities for computer science and technology, I propose a partnership between the federal government and state governments. The federal government will have to make a substantial financial investment in these institutions, primarily involved in construction costs and creating endowments.[9] A state government will provide a track of usable land for the university to be constructed upon and grow. The federal government will provide the initial funding for the endowment with additional future payments made in decreasing amounts until the land grant university is no longer funded and financially supported by the federal government. After this point with the federal government is reached, the maintenance and responsibility of the land grant university will be the responsibility of the corresponding state government. The federal government will also contribute to the initial cost of construction which will be shared with the state government. Each public land grant university for computer science and technology will be a mutual investment by state governments and the federal government.

---

[9] Endowing these public land grant universities will make each university more self-sufficient and defray the future maintenance cost to the government.

The mammoth underperformance of the kindergarten through secondary school education system across the United States in educating American children to think and for future career opportunities has many causes. Adequate financial funding is certainly a necessity that is missing from many local school systems across the United States and children need an adequate level and quality of resources to utilize in order to develop to their full potential, but we should not make the mistake of placing the burden of improving children's educational performance on financial funding alone. Highlighting the disparity in funding between school systems is the easiest way and most political powerful way to advocate for education reform, but we will do a grave mistake to focus solely or over weight financial funding as the cause and solution to our education problems. Many other factors play into the United States' failure to create a better education system, one of the largest determining factors in a child's educational success is the value placed on education by their family, in essence, family values. Along with family income, parents' education levels are highly correlated with the success of their children educationally. Given that one's parents or authority figures play perhaps the biggest role in shaping a child's values, it is no surprise that educated parents who value education and instil an importance for education within their children are overwhelmingly parents of successful children both educationally and economically. If one looks at the two most economically and educationally successful immigrant groups by culture in the United States since 1965, one finds that cultures that places great value on education and success in educational pursuits produce the two most economically successful culture groups; South Asian and East Asian Americans.

With their well know 'Tiger Moms' becoming an easily recognizable pop culture reference, East Asian parents have become easily recognized for the value they place on education and the degree that it is instilled in their children. Once the state of California lifted their affirmative action policy at their state universities, East Asian and South Asian American student enrollment made a significant increase. It is no coincidence that East Asian and South Asian Americans are overrepresented in undergraduate institutions and professional graduate schools such as medical schools, law schools, and business schools. The cultural importance placed education by East Asian and South Asian families has produced tangible results in graduate school enrollment and along with higher education levels, individual economic success. One cannot objectively ignore the fact of the value East and South Asian American cultures put on education towards their individual economic success.[10]

---

[10] Given the conclusion reached that the East Asian and South Asian American cultures put a greater emphasis on education than other cultures, one may find oneself confronted with a question; Why then do India and China lag behind the United States in many education criteria such as school attendance rates, educational investment in real terms and per capita, and in general economic success? A very good question indeed. First, it is important to make the distinction between East Asian/South Asian cultures and East Asian American/South Asian American cultures. East Asian Americans and South Asian Americans certainly borrow a great deal from the geographic areas of their cultural roots, but they are also living and interacting in the United States, which undoubtedly influences and in part constructs their cultural experience. So drawing a direct parallel between East Asian American/South Asian American culture and East Asian/South Asian culture is not an apples for apples comparison. Second, there is a disparity that should be accounted for between China/India and the United States in terms of

The value East Asian and South Asian American cultures place on education is a great American success story that 'feels good' to hold up and pronounce as well as bringing up few issues of current popular political correctness and niceties. We must also correctly diagnose cultures that do not value education, in order to better craft solutions for all of America's children. If we become beholden to current popular political correctness and are too worried about not remotely offending any culture group, we risk falsely diagnosing problems and failing to provide better education for those Americans affected. Without singling out any particular American cultural groups, there are certain American cultural groups who do not place the same value on education as other groups. As a result over decades of placing less emphasis on education culturally, these cultural groups are often more highly correlated with low income earnings.[11] Considering that local, state, and federal governments in the United States already have many programs aimed at giving aid to low income citizens in a variety of ways, a tremendous opportunity is presented to utilize existing government programs to aid in educational development. We have an opportunity to make government programs more efficient without increasing their cost. If the United States is to meet all of its large outstanding financial obligations, citizens cannot count on an increase, in real terms, in funding for government programs in the future. I believe policy maker will have to turn towards efficiency to achieve any gains in effectiveness of government programs.

Therefore as a general strategy, I advocate utilizing existing government programs or in the utilization of new government programs to incorporate education and educational development into the end goal of each program. Shifting existing funding to new outlets that incorporate new aspects while still dispensing funds to those citizens targeted and setting new conditions for government aide if done in an imaginative ways have the potential to increase aide to low income citizens without drastic increases in government funding cost. For example, welfare benefits and food stamps given to parents with children can be linked to their children's school attendance rate. A similar program linking government aid to school attendance rates has yielded substantial increases in the percentage of children attending school in Brazil.[12] Providing more incentives for low income individuals to send their children to school is a low cost addition to our existing efforts as well as targeting a demographic of children who have the lowest school attendance rates in the United States. A further addition could be to redirect a portion of aid, whether through direct cash payments or the food stamp programs, towards providing food at schools. A portion of that money could be sent to schools so schools can

---

per capita income, quality of educational institutions, general economic development, sophistication of the public sector and public services, corruption, rule of law, etc. Considering the differences between China/India and the United States in these previously mentioned areas, there are many factors that enable a cultural value to achieve higher levels of success.

[11] This statement in no way attributes causation or the majority of causation for a specific American cultural groups lack of economic success to their value of education. Placing value on education is simply one of the factors to be considered.

[12] Note that Brazil is staring form a much lower point of economic development than the United States and gains will be much larger in nominal terms as a result.

provide breakfast, lunch, and an after school mean to children, directly tying government aid to schools. Children will have to attend school in order to receive their aid. With advances in technology over the past 10 years, most American schools provide their students with identification cards similar to driver's licenses. These identification cards are used for entry into the school and most often kids can purchase a school meal plan and/or put money on their school cards which in turn are used to pay for meals at school. Government funds for low income students could be supplied directly to the students' account at the school which would enable them to visibly pay for their meals with their student card without the social stigma of visibly using food stamps or some form of government aid. Also, providing meals through the school gives the government more control over what children eat. The government can guarantee healthy options for three meals a day, ensuring the student receives their daily amount of nutrition, with the potential of increasing the health of American children. Schools providing meals to low income children also relieves the burden from parents who are often working long hours and may not have the time or energy to research the nutritional facts behind healthy means or buy healthy ingredients. Programs like these will be essential in a future where the United States is operating with a diminished financial capacity. Programs will have to become more efficient. We will have to focus more on what we do with our resources than on the level of our resources.

Throughout the kindergarten through secondary school education levels, the federal government has very little control over individual school system funding. At best the federal government can exert some control over school systems by raising standards. The main culprit behind the lack of federal government control and influence over individual school system funding is the extreme decentralization of America's school systems. The federal government has very few ways of influencing local communities or bringing pressure on them. The most effective tool the federal government has at its disposal is the federal purse, funding for state and local government programs, ranging from highway funding to Medicare and Medicaid funding. The federal government provides billions of dollars to states mostly in partial and sometimes full funding of state programs. By utilizing funding for state and local programs as leverage, the federal government can influence local governments. If the federal government wanted states and localities to contribute more towards a program the federal government could withhold funding for other programs until states and localities agreed to provide more funding for the program in question. The federal government did this in the 1980's in order to achieve an increase in state legal drinking ages. In the 1980's the federal government withheld highway funding from states that did not maintain a legal drinking age of 21 years. No state held out for even an entire year. If this was achieved with just withholding highway funding, the added pressure of withholding funding from other programs would bring even more pressure onto the shoulders of state and local governments.

In order to achieve increased funding for individual school systems across the United States, I advocate that the federal government increase the amount of educational funding to states and localities along with increased educational standards and practices, conditional upon states and localities increasing their funding for school systems. If the federal government increases funding to states and localities for local school systems, the federal government becomes a partner with state and local governments. However, the increase in federal funding to states and localities for education should not be drastic. In the future the United States will have to operate with a relatively diminished financial capacity. Therefore the bulk of increased funding for school systems needs to come from local governments and to a lesser extent state governments.

Along with increased federal funding for local education systems, the federal government will also require higher educational standards and certain educational practices changed or added. Given the nature and rate of technological advancement in recent years and the increasing dependence of businesses and people on technology, the government should mandate a curriculum that incorporates computer science and programming classes for all students. Most American high schools require two years of study of a foreign language; a similar requirement can be made for the study of computer programming languages. Education experts can decide what age range is best for learning computer programming languages, although I would lean towards a much earlier introduction to programming than high school, ideally in grammar school. The standards for teaching qualifications need to be increased as well, along with a much needed increase in teacher pay. For secondary school teachers, a requirement of holding a bachelor's degree in the subject they will instruct will be a requirement. Other changes to the standards required to teach should be implanted as well, with the guise of attracting and obtaining better more effective teachers in American school systems. To compensate for these changes and to attract more qualified individuals to the teaching profession, teaching salaries should be doubled at least. Teaching is one of, if not the noblest profession an individual can undertake, we should reward our teachers financially for their service and place a financial weight on education in our society.

Other standards that should be adopted involve the increased utilization of technology in class rooms to give teachers faster and in certain instances instantaneous feedback. Teachers should not have to wait until the end of the semester or school year to receive the results of standardized tests, by then it is too late to help their students. With increased use of technology, more timely feedback can allow teachers to correct their lesson plans to better accommodate the needs of their students during the school year.

On a larger macro level, our conception of the school year needs to change. Too many public school systems in the United States have a mandatory limit of days they must remain open, which springs from a conception of education that treats time as an independent variable and results as a dependent variable, x input of hours equals y return on results. Educational results rarely work in this fashion. We need to conceptually change results as the input. The duration of the school year should be dependent on the results and learning of students. Increasingly, better performing school around the world are moving towards year round education, conducting classes on Saturdays, adding an hour to the school day, and many other practices with the goal of achieving results for their students. In a globally competitive world, United States students must not be shackled by old ways of thinking and comfortable practices of the past. We need to adapt to a changing world that is more competitive, if we fail to do this we put our future workforce at a competitive disadvantage.

While these educational reforms will vastly help American students, there will almost certainly be without question, large levels of hostility in local communities to increasing taxes to pay for these educational advances. Simply put, people do not like to pay more of their income to the government. Even with the increase in educational funding from the federal government, local communities will most likely not be swayed in support. The federal government will have to utilize its power of the purse to coerce local communities and states to pay their portion of the proposed increase in educational spending. The federal government should withhold all educational funding as well as highway funding and any other funding for state and local programs until local governments and state governments acquiesce to the increases in funding advocated by the federal government. The cost of making up the loss of federal educational funding and highway funding alone will greatly exceed the proposed increase in educational funding to be paid by local governments and states. Local governments may be able to hold out longer than state governments, but the increased venerability of state governments is an asset to be utilized against local governments. Currently, many states have serious budget problems, given the federal government's suspension of funding more bite. The federal government can then exert more influence on state governments to place more pressure on local governments through a variety of means to force local governments to acquiesce, raise taxes, and increase funding for schools. While the plan laid out above is incredibly draconian in its execution, it however is the most viable and effective way for the federal government to achieve lasting and sustainable change to kindergarten through secondary school education systems through the United States. This plan will require elected public servants, with no small degree of courage and the stomach for being disliked. This elected public servant will without question have to expend a great deal of political capital in enacting this plan. I do believe that the results to be gained by this plan far outweigh the costs of not bettering the education system in the United States.

The United States need to improve its education system to be competitive in the world we currently inhabit and any future world. As other nations grow economically and move out of the third world, American students and workers will encounter ever increasing workplace competition, creating downward pressure on wages. We must give our students and workers the ability to compete with competition from around the world. The United States was one of the first industrialized nations to embrace universal grammar through secondary school education and our universities have become the envy of the world, our past educational advantages have contributed greatly to the economic, cultural, and technological supremacy the United States enjoys today. If we are to maintain our place at the top we will have to embrace changes and improvements in our education system.

Healthcare

The current healthcare law, the Affordable Healthcare Act[13] passed in 2010, is an
admirable attempt at creating a national healthcare system that achieves universal coverage in a
sustainable and nationally affordable way. It is admirable in its intentions but not its execution.
The Affordable Healthcare Act of 2010 is a deeply flawed law that does not adequately address
several core issues of the healthcare debate in a realistic fashion. The Affordable Healthcare Act
is at best a bad patch on an already bad system. In addition to being inadequate for our
healthcare demands it may have many negative consequences in many aspects of the United
States economy and further divisions in American society. If the United States wants to move
forward with the Affordable Healthcare Act, many changes of a radical nature will need to be
implemented in the near future in order to make the practical application of the law live up to the
admirable goals of those who authored the Affordable Healthcare Act. Or the United States will
need to produce a new, separate law to address our national healthcare concerns, in the process
making the Affordable Healthcare Act a worthy attempt assigned to the historical scrap heap. If
the United States is serious about addressing its myriad healthcare concerns, one of the two
above prescribed courses of action will need to unfold. Given the relative weakness and deep
structural flaws of the current Affordable Healthcare Act, I advocate a completely new law to
address our nation's healthcare concerns structured very differently from the Affordable
Healthcare Act. I will discuss our current national healthcare concerns and challenges
confronting the United States, then outline the structural and societal deficiencies and merits of
the Affordable Healthcare Act, and finally I will outline a general proposal for a framework of
guidelines for a new national healthcare system. I want to iterate again, that these are ideas
worth discussing and that they should not be taken as a finished product that is actionable in any
way.

First, allow me to make a point regarding the absurd light I have witnessed many
discussions on the Affordable Healthcare Act devolve into and be consumed by to a pointless
end. I have come across a peculiar situation, unfortunately all too often, where any criticism of
the general details or structure of the Affordable Healthcare Act is met with counterpoint, 'You

---

[13] I will endeavor to refer to the healthcare law signed into law by President Obama in 2010 by its abbreviated title,
The Affordable Healthcare Act. I will endeavor to not refer to the Affordable Healthcare Act as 'Obamacare.' I will
do this in order to avoid any built in hostility or admiration the term may bring to the table. Also because I would
like to see politics become more civil and pragmatic, and less dependent on emotive appeal, political spin, and
demagoguery. When discussing the Affordable Healthcare Act we must discuss the law on its merits from its text,
not on the author or our opinions of the author and/or the author's political ideology, lest those outside influences
corrupt our interpretations and we become beholden to them.

don't want everyone to have healthcare,' or a similar phrase producing the same effect. I believe this rhetoric is unproductive for uneristic debate and is dangerous for our democracy. For all intents and purposes, everyone outside of a few radical far right wing ideologues wants every citizen of the United States to have access to affordable healthcare. The idea that one side or the other seriously doesn't want American citizens to have healthcare is a rhetoric tool designed for emotional appeal without logical or substantial grounding. We can all agree that we all want everyone in the United States to have healthcare. I defy one to find a serious American politician that readily admits to not wanting American citizens to have healthcare. If found they would be the rarest of a newly discovered species. A person may disagree with the methods of how the Affordable Healthcare Act achieves universal coverage and changes the American healthcare landscape AND still want to want every American to have healthcare coverage. The only disagreement lies in the methods used to achieve the goal of universal healthcare, not in the end goal itself. Therefore, in serious discussions regarding the merits of the Affordable Healthcare Act, we can refrain from making the absurd assertion that simply because someone disagrees with the mechanics of the Affordable Healthcare Act they do not want people to have healthcare. We should not mistake criticism of the means and details for rejection of the end goal.

Another undesirable consequence of the above described line of thinking is that it damages uneristic debate, which is vital for a representative democracy built with the concept of debate as a core tenant. A functioning democracy should be able to entertain debates on the merits of a law in a public forum. Opposition to certain parts of a law and critiquing them in public debate is part of American democracy and provides an avenue for dissenting voices. Debate also allows a proposed law to undergo the necessary criticism and revisions needed to improve the law and reach enough of a consensus for widespread adoption. As I have witnessed often, the moment a person makes a counter point to criticism of the workings of the Affordable Health Care Act with the a similar comment to, "You don't want everyone to have healthcare," the debate is effectively over. In order for the political process to work in the United States in a fashion that respects the rights of the party not in power, an avenue for discussion and debate needs to be provided and nurtured. While many may disagree with criticism of a particular laws merits and functional details, it is still vital to respect and provide an avenue for the opinions of dissenters. By denying this avenue to critics of the Affordable Healthcare Act we are limiting our democracy. The above point made in this paragraph applies not only to Congressional discussions, but more importantly to interpersonal discussions between non-representative citizens, in coffee shops, university classrooms, and other public forums found in daily life. While seeming not as important, one cannot dispute that the vast majority of public debate, by quantity, happens outside of Congress and helps form the national character. Why don't we build our national character on a sound foundation.

Surveying our current healthcare landscape in February of 2014 before the implantation of the Affordable Healthcare Act, it becomes clear the United States does not currently have a 'healthcare system' in the traditional sense of the word. We have a healthcare market, which entails the benefits and costs of a market based system. Healthcare costs are set by the collective decisions of the market participants and most healthcare infrastructure is private. As opposed to a government run healthcare system like Britain's National Healthcare Service or Canada's healthcare system in which most infrastructure is operated by the national government which sets prices as well. A single payer government run system allows for price controls, but is dependent on the competency of those public servants running the system. Generally markets respond to changing circumstances, such as increasing pay to attract workers to jobs with shortages, faster than government run systems and more efficiently allocate resources.

Our healthcare market is augmented by the practice of employer provided or subsidized healthcare plans, which theoretically serves to partially defray the cost of healthcare to the individual.[14] Corporations and other business have been providing the bulk of Americans healthcare coverage since the advent of price freezes enacted during World War II. With millions of men under military service and government price and wage freezes imposed by the United States government for the war effort, business needed a way to attract and retain workers beyond the usual peacetime practice of raising wages. The most effective way they found was offering fringe benefits to employees, which were not subject to limitations by the US government. One of the most popular and effective benefits was the offering of healthcare coverage to workers. The duration of the war and the relative strength of the United States economy which produced tremendous financial gains for American firms[15], made this practice ingrained in the American corporate structure and worker expectations. This practice of employer provided or subsidized healthcare has endured to our present day. Objectively this practice of employer provided healthcare seems to be inefficient for corporations, workers, and insurance providers. Providing healthcare for workers, especially in a time period when healthcare costs are increasing at over twice the rate of inflation, is a growing and burdensome cost for employers, that isn't abundantly transparent to the casual surveyor. It makes employing American workers more costly, for example wages for the average Canadian worker are higher than wages for the average American worker, but Canadian workers are less costly to employ than American workers. The main culprit for this cost differential between Canadian and American workers is the healthcare costs associated with employing Americans. Healthcare costs are also a variable cost largely beyond the control of employers, wage costs are much easier to plan for and give employers total control over that expense. Adding in the historically difficult to predict long-term cost of providing subsidizing healthcare for retired employees, healthcare costs can become a major expenditure for employers. Providing healthcare coverage for employees is burdensome cost for employers that make American business less competitive

---

[14] Theoretically this benefit is taken out of wages and can be used as an excuse for not increasing wages if healthcare costs have accelerated faster than wage growth. Under a theoretical situation, if healthcare costs were no longer required of employers, wages would rise to reflect this change.
[15] Especially in comparison to war torn Europe and Japan. There was virtually no economic rival to the immediate post United States.

in comparison to international competition who do not have to provide healthcare for their employees.

The employer provided healthcare system also decreases mobility within the labor market hurting the efficiency of the American labor market by tying employees to their current forms of employment. Workers are less likely to take risks and leave their current jobs as well as staying longer than is optimal because of worries about obtaining health insurance, especially if an opportunity does not work out. Workers flexibility within the labor market is decreased by the employer provided healthcare system as well as creating a less dynamic labor market for employers. Another consideration of the employer provided healthcare system dependent on workers leaving their current jobs, affects one of the United States great strengths, our entrepreneurs. The prospect of losing your healthcare coverage may be a factor that makes the decision to leave one's current job and start a new company that much more difficult. It may also dissuade workers from quitting their current jobs and joining a startup company, therefore depriving the next Google of talented employees. In short, removing the connection between employer and healthcare will make the US labor market more dynamic and fluid, producing a better result for employers, workers, and entrepreneurship in the United States.

The current[16] healthcare market in the United States has created a bureaucratic triangle between insurance providers, employers, and individuals which has produced an unnecessary middle man, the employer. Instead of a direct relationship between the average citizen and their health insurance provider, the citizen must obtain health insurance from their employer and negotiate through their employer. The employer as the middle man between citizen and health insurance provider creates more bureaucracy in an industry that is already rife with bureaucracy and paperwork. On any level, an extra middle man complicates the health insurance process for hard working Americans and slows down the ability of health insurance providers to quickly respond to the needs of the citizens they cover. To put it simply, by placing the American business as an unnecessary middle man in our healthcare system, the United States has made a less efficient healthcare system. A more efficient system that has a direct relationship between insurance provider and individual reduces a middle man, creates less bureaucracy, paper work, and makes interaction between individual and insurance provider much easier.

Given all of this, we are left at an impasse, do we want to keep the employer provided healthcare system and work within it towards a solution or do we want to create a new system independent of employers. The authors of the Affordable Healthcare Act have clearly chosen the former path.

While containing many significant flaws, the Affordable Healthcare Act does have several effective functional changes worth keeping in one form or another. The advent of health insurance exchanges, allowing young adults to stay on their parents medical insurance plans until

---

[16] 'Current' defined as pre-Affordable Healthcare Act implementation

the age of 26, and banning health insurance providers from charging higher premiums for those with adverse pre-existing health conditions are examples of effective structural changes to the state of the healthcare environment in the United States before the advent of the Affordable Healthcare Act.

The concept of creating an exchange for healthcare plans is a very effective improvement on the current listless state of information one finds upon undertaking to identify, let alone research health insurance plans in our current system. Today, before the implementation of the Affordable Healthcare Act, a prospective health insurance buyer is confronted with the polar opposite of information transparency about health insurance plans. One is left to one's own devices and must search in a healthcare world without any guiding or formal structure. The person who seeks to purchase health insurance must peruse many health insurance company websites, make their own comparisons, and identify as many health insurance providers as possible in a completely diffuse, decentralized health insurance market. This daunting task is made possible by the lack of any formal structure or regulation of the healthcare insurance market. This informal, decentralized market is highly inefficient for disseminating information about health insurance and providing timely and effortless connections between prospective health insurance buyers and health insurance firms. To draw a comparative example, imagine a world in which stock exchanges do not exist. Now one is tasked with buying stocks for a diversified portfolio. One must identify available stocks to buy, ascertain historical stock price movements for each stock, calculate a rate of return on each stock, and compare stocks to each other in a comparative analysis, all with the goal of creating a portfolio which one can earn a return above the market return[17]. Outperforming the market is a difficult task today even with modern stock exchanges and transparency of information, woe betide the individual who must attempt the same task in a world without a centralized hub of information that makes comparative analysis exponentially easier and substantially less time consumer, i.e. a stock exchange. Given the readily apparent and truly incredible advantages that stock exchanges provide over the alternative lack thereof, in terms of increased information accessibility and ease of comparative analysis, it seems quite odd that we have not utilized exchanges for other aspect of the United States economy. Exchanges should be a politically tolerable idea given the overwhelming wide acceptance and use of stock exchanges. A healthcare exchange will allow prospective health insurance buyers to more easily discover and compare health insurance plans, making the process substantially less time consuming. Exchanges will bring the full effect of market forces to bear, forcing health insurers to compete against each other, which is made much easier by the fact that consumers can more easily compare prices. Without exchanges insurers can exploit the lack of comparative information available to consumers to charge higher prices.

While the idea of a healthcare exchange is an effective one and should be adopted, the affordable healthcare act employs the idea in such a way that it creates unnecessary and burdensome complexities for the United States healthcare system, one of the many flaws of the

---

[17] Provided one can gather enough data in this neo-world without a stock exchange to calculate the market return.

affordable healthcare act. It is a great step that the affordable healthcare act employs exchanges to list health insurance, the benefits have been outlined in the preceding paragraph, but the affordable healthcare act decentralizes the exchange idea and allows each state to construct their own exchange. Theoretically there could be 50 healthcare exchanges across the United States, each operating independently from each other and potentially each operating with different rules and procedures. This lack of a centralized system creates asymmetric problems in the aggregate resulting from different policies and rules across states. This regionalization of healthcare has detrimental effects for labor market flexibility and the ability of workers to relocate for new job opportunities. Policies that apply in certain states may not apply in other states. Creating a centralized system for healthcare, for example a single national exchange, would be incredibly more efficient, uniform, and support labor market flexibility.

Another flaw keeping the affordable healthcare act from becoming truly transformative healthcare legislation is its acceptance and promotion of the employer provided healthcare system and relationship. As mentioned earlier, the employer provided healthcare system is rife with inefficiencies and hurts labor market flexibility. In addition, the affordable healthcare act has requirements for small business to cover more employees, creating increased costs for small business owners and entrepreneurs. Entrepreneurship has been important to the economic development of the United States, creating many of the United States' current largest employers and providing a pathway of social mobility for hardworking, ingenuous Americans. The affordable healthcare act is increasing the costs of starting a company in the United States, especially for the majority of entrepreneurs who are not backed by millions in venture capital funding. In order to compete in an increasingly competitive global economy, the United States will need its entrepreneurs and needs to give them the best chance of succeeding.

The affordable healthcare act will achieve an increase in the percentage of Americans covered by health insurance, which is a wonderful accomplishment, but it does not at all adequately address the increasing and projected to increase costs to the United States government, especially considering that many of the newly insured will be insured by and expansion of Medicare and Medicaid. Much of the projected cost savings in the affordable healthcare act rely on projected efficiency gains in the healthcare industry. Basing cost saving projections on efficiency gains is a bit suspect given the historical difficulty in predicting efficiency gains and that those gains are assumed and outside of any control by the government. Savings by efficiency may very well come about, but the large gains projected under the affordable healthcare act are unreliable and seem the product of wishful thinking. In addition, the affordable healthcare act does not address in a real way the increasing cost of healthcare to the United States government. The cost of Medicare and Medicaid are predicted to increase at similar rates under the affordable healthcare act as without. The increasing cost of healthcare entitlements to the United States government is projected by the congressional budget office to become greater than military spending and a drastic burden on the United States government, providing less money to spend on education and infrastructure. The affordable healthcare act only address one side of the healthcare debate in the United States, increasing coverage, it would be better if it also addressed the cost of healthcare to the United States government.

Finally, the long-term societal impacts of the affordable healthcare act may serve to further divide the United States. Much has been made in the media of the wealth gap between the wealthiest and least wealthy in American society, and more importantly the shrinking size proportionally of the middle class creating greater class divides in the United States. While much attention is hyped for ratings, there is a very real danger of creating a more divided society and this divide is increasingly being defined on education lines. In an economy where agriculture and manufacturing no longer provide a significant proportion of jobs, services and skills become much more important. Having a university education is increasingly important. Social scientist have identified educational attainment as the greatest indicator of economic success, health, and living standards in the United States. The United States is moving towards a society that is increasingly being divided by educational attainment. I believe the affordable healthcare act will increase this social divide further, primarily because it keeps the employer provided healthcare system as the primary avenue for obtaining healthcare in the United States. Very well educated people have better chances of obtaining jobs with employers who will pay for high quality healthcare as a benefit. They do not have to seek health insurance from an exchange. Those without an education who cannot obtain a highly coveted job with a firm that provides health insurance will be forced to seek healthcare on an exchange. Healthcare exchanges will be utilities primarily by the uneducated. Perhaps a stigma will evolve for those who purchase healthcare from an exchange, I hope not. There is a real danger in the affordable healthcare act further defining the socio-economic divide in the United States. For those who are concerned with the socio-economic dynamics of American society, they should consider the social implications of the affordable healthcare act.

Given the state of congress at the time, politically the affordable healthcare act was surely the most feasible and less disruptive option, which is amazing given the extreme lack of support and opposition is entailed. American citizens, for the most part like, other country's citizens around the world, are uncomfortable with drastic change and adapting to a new societal paradigm. It is unsurprising that politicians worried about reelection prospects chose the less disruptive and more comfortable option. The safe approach would be appropriate if it achieved effective reform, but with the Affordable Healthcare Act we are left without effective healthcare reform. American elected officials have chosen comfortable mediocrity over difficult effectiveness. The American people deserve better from their elected officials.

After highlighting the inadequacies of the pre-Affordable Healthcare Act environment in the United States and of the Affordable Healthcare Act in addressing the many demands of the American healthcare landscape, I will present some ideas and the general framework for a healthcare system that I believe will better serve the United States. Again, these are ideas intended more for thought and rumination than a finalized plan that is ready to be adopted. They are too general and need to be worked through further to be immediately actionable. Hopefully they will provide some food for thought for the existing conversation.

As highlighted previously, the employer provided healthcare system is inefficient and in the guise of the affordable healthcare act may actually increase socio-economic divisions in society. I propose completely removing the employer provided healthcare system so that no one in the United States will receive their healthcare from their employers. Removing the implicit obligation of employers to provide health insurance for their employees will have the same effect as a tax break for employers and make American workers cheaper to hire. It will make American firms more competitive around the world because a variable cost much outside the control of the firm is eliminated and it will make American workers more attractive to hire by domestic and foreign firms. The benefits to the economic competitiveness of the United States are real.

In exchange of the employer provided healthcare system, I believe the United States should adopt a system that brings the best of the free market and government systems together. I propose setting up one national healthcare exchange that every health insurance provider will be required to list on as well as the United States government creating a government run insurance agency that will provide multiple insurance options for those who are priced out of the exchange.

A national healthcare exchange is superior to collective state exchanges because it brings national market instead of individual state market forces to bear lowering prices through greater competition, provides better mobility in the labor market, has a set rules and regulation system that applies throughout the entire country, and will have more than enough participants to make the exchange viable. As discussed earlier in regards to the current pre-affordable healthcare act system, market forces can be utilized to great effect; competition by insurers lowers prices and markets adjust faster to shortages or gluts in the industry as with creating higher salaries for nurses during a time of nurse shortages. A national healthcare exchange brings the benefits of market forces to work in the healthcare industry. With the majority of Americans buying their health insurance on a national exchange instead of through their employers, market forces can still provide their positive benefits to consumers in the healthcare industry. Also with the majority of Americans buying their health insurance from a national exchange, it provides a much deeper pool for the exchange than any individual state exchange could ever produce. This much much deeper pool for the national exchange will alleviate any fears that currently exist about enough people buying from exchanges to make them viable, after all, they will not have any other choice but to buy from the national exchange. Also with every insurance company forced to list on a national exchange, greater competition will be more effective in prices than a state exchange's capacity to lower prices.

A single national exchange will produce the result of anyone who purchases health insurance from the exchange operating under the same rules and regulations regardless of where in the United States they are living when purchasing their health insurance. This makes it much easier for Americans to move between states when they do not have to worry about meeting requirements or regulations for a particular state. In addition to a general uniform set of regulations, removing the employer provided healthcare system for an exchange will provide an environment where workers are more likely to leave existing jobs for new ones, creating a more efficient labor market. In the current employer provided healthcare system, employees may be reticent about quitting their jobs for new ones with the worry of losing their health insurance. (The dilemma of paying for health insurance when in between jobs is a real challenge and will be addressed later in this essay) Taking a job that also includes a degree of quality of health insurance will no longer be a consideration. Entrepreneurs will no longer have to factor in the cost of employees health coverage when starting the next Google or Nike and they may leave their current occupations to start their new firms without worrying about losing their employer provided healthcare. (Again the dilemma of paying for their health insurance in between will be addressed later in this essay) The multiple benefits of utilizing a national exchange are very persuasive.

Another benefit of a national health insurance exchange, without employer provided health insurance, is that it does not create the necessity of requiring all citizens to have health insurance or to fine those citizens who choose not have health insurance. Even with maintaining an employer provided health insurance system, a national health insurance exchange will have the numbers necessary to make it viable without fining those who choose not to have health insurance. And with all those who previously received their health insurance from their employers, purchasing health insurance from the national exchange, the national exchange is further augmented and is made even more viable. Americans, like many in other nations, do not like to be told what to do or to have restrictions placed on their behavior. I suspect most hostility to restrictions is mostly philosophical in nature and not actually derived from any physical discomfort these restrictions cause in the routine of daily life. Nonetheless, removing the requirement of obtaining health insurance will ease opposition to healthcare reform by removing a philosophical rallying point for the opposition.

A national health insurance exchange will most likely succeed in lowering the prices paid by consumers out of competition, but prices may not be low enough for every American. A person's healthcare is too important to leave to the market alone. Having a healthy workforce is important to the productivity of the American economy. I propose the United States government create a government run health insurance company, which will offer multiple plans, to provide health insurance for those few who are priced out of the national healthcare exchange. Non-government health insurance firms do not have the ability to operate at a reduced profit or at a loss as can the United States government. The United States government can utilize economic demographic data as well as historical price analysis of the national health insurance exchange to set prices properly for those priced out of the national health insurance. To qualify for the different government health insurance plans, one will have to meet certain income criteria, so those earning below designated income levels will qualify for different government health insurance plans. The government will determine these income levels from economic demographic data.

I propose the United States government health insurance company provide at least three different options for paid health insurance and one option that is free. The free option will be open to those earning below a certain income threshold in order to allow only those who need it to have access and diminish the cost to the United States government. This free option will only provide the bare essentials of health coverage, it will not be nearly as high quality as what one could purchase on the national health insurance exchange. This will be achieved by reducing choices. One on free government health insurance will be able to see a doctor and get all the treatments they need, but they will not have a choice in which doctor they are able to see. They will be assigned a doctor by their insurance and that will be their only option, same with seeing specialists. The free government health insurance option will provide all the necessary care one needs, but without choice. I liken the free option to a used Toyota corolla. It is not flashy at all and without creature comforts, but it is more than capable of getting one from point A to point B. Using economic demographic information, the United States government will price the three paid government health insurance options and the income thresholds for each accordingly so that they accommodate the needs of those who cannot afford to purchase a private plan from the national health insurance exchange but earn too much for the free government insurance options. The government insurance options are meant to augment the health insurance exchanges and fill in the gaps at the bottom for those priced out of the exchange.

Under this new scenario, Medicare and Medicaid will cease to exist and their previous users will enroll in either an insurance plan from the national health insurance exchange or one of the government health insurance plans. The United States government forming a health insurance company provides the government with the same negotiation power with hospitals, doctors, and pharmaceutical providers that private health insurance companies currently enjoy. The United States government, backed by the taxpayers, will be able to leverage a higher financial security rating and a nationwide pool of participants, comprised of those utilizing government insurance plans, to negotiate great rates and conditions for itself and its participants. By entering the market as an insurance company, the United States government will be able to negotiate and gain an offensive power in controlling costs that the United States government currently does not enjoy with Medicare and Medicaid. Within the context of government provided healthcare, a government insurance firm operating in the market place provides the government with the greatest ability to control costs. We must not be under any illusions though, creating a government health insurance company will require the recruitment of qualified staff and the nationwide infrastructure to serve participants and fulfill obligations and operations.

It is important to note that there is a precedent of the United States government operating firms in the general market place already. The United States government operates banks and insurance firms serving military veterans and their families. They provide many much needed services to military veterans, from mortgages to auto insurance. A viable precedent has been established in the United States already.

While I believe the general framework described above is the most efficient system for creating a comprehensive healthcare system in the United States, it is not without its faults. Requiring most people to purchase their insurance from a national exchange, even with less expensive health insurance costs as a result of the exchange, is asking most people to pay more for their health insurance from the employer provided system. Given that firms can no longer offer health insurance as a fringe benefit, it seems reasonable that firms would raise wages to attract top talent and that hopefully wage increases offset the new cost of health insurance purchased from an exchange. This may not happen however, wage increases could not be consummate with new health insurance costs. In all likelihood adopting the healthcare system advocated for in this essay will require an additional cost to most Americans. Ideas designed to save the government in healthcare cost may actually turn out to be more expansive than previously thought. Many who opt for government health insurance plans may be dissatisfied with the extent of their coverage in comparison to plans available on the national health insurance exchange. From a political feasibly standpoint, creating a government health insurance firm may not be possible. Given the current extreme partisanship enjoyed by both main political parties and the republican opposition to the relatively benign affordable healthcare act, it is more likely than not that a healthcare law with a provision for a government health insurance firm will not come close to passing. Under any national healthcare system there will most assuredly be very passionate and vocal detractors, as the current pre-affordable healthcare act system and the affordable healthcare system have experienced, but passionate dissent should not be automatically confused with well thought out identified systemic flaws.

I believe the national healthcare system I have outlined in this essay to be the best, most efficient system in general that the United States could employ. I believe that it combines the best of a market system with the best of a government provided system. Hopefully this essay will encourage discussion on the topic of healthcare reform beyond a mere debate on the affordable healthcare act or nothing new at all. The affordable healthcare act is an admirable effort at healthcare reform, but I believe the United States can and must do better.

Gun Control

Few areas of discussion are more divisive and provoke stronger reactions than the current debate about gun control and the legal status of firearms in the United States. A partly subjective debate about the interpretation and limits of the 2th amendment to the Constitution seems never ending with few chances of compromise on the horizon. After the horrific events of Sandy Hook, Aura, and other tragic shootings, the call for gun control in the United States is perhaps nearing an apex. In the spirit of this series of essays, I will argue that the current gun control debate within the United States does not address the core gun control issues that affect the vast majority of people and shooting deaths within the United States. I will argue that the current debate does not discuss or aim to correct the fact that the overwhelming majority of gun crimes within the US involve illegally obtained guns, over 80%. In addition I will also make a case for a political compromise that both the current moderate right and left can endorse that addresses the core issues behind most shooting incidents and specifically the shooting incidents that happen every day in America's inner cities. Before I continue, I would like to make an appeal to logic and to not become beholden to anecdotal evidence. This author believes that any gun control measure that does not address the horrific state of illegal guns in the United States is a pyrrhic victory at best.

The current debate within the majority of the United States and especially our elected leaders around the topic of gun control focuses on creating more stringent requirements for obtaining legal firearms. After the tragedies of Aura, CO and Sandy Hook elementary, it is easy to see why there is a strong public reaction towards these measures. After all, each incident involved a deranged individual, possibly suffering from mental health issues, who utilized legally purchased guns to devastating effect. A national gun registry, limits on ammunition containers[18], more extensive background checks, and longer waiting periods may affect those seeking to do harm to others who decide to obtain their firearms legally. If only the majority of crimes involving firearms occurred with legally obtained guns. The sad reality is that over 80%

---

[18] Upon inspection, this seems to be an arbitrary restriction. For example, removing 9 round clips in exchange for 7 round clips, seems an arbitrary distinction. What is to stop a person from buying two 7 round clips?

of crimes involving guns occur with illegally obtained guns[19]. Therefore, when one takes a series stab at curtailing gun crimes in the United States, a policy that only focuses on illegal guns has the potential to affect at most 20% of gun crimes in the United States. A national solution that affects at most 20% of the problem can hardly be considered an adequate solution. Further evidence is given by the recent relaxation of gun control laws in Washington D.C., still the nations harshest. For many years D.C. had one of the highest crime rates within the United States, overall and involving firearms. In the first year after Washington D.C. residents were allowed to purchase hand guns, there was one single recorded shooting involving a legally purchased gun. There was no discernable increase in crimes involving guns that could be attributed to the lifting of Washington D.C.'s previous firearms ban.

Another important consideration when crafting a well thought out national policy to decrease gun crimes should be how the plan is viewed and considered in the media as well. We should not correlate greater media attention of certain types of gun crimes with a notion of prevalence or frequency of those types of crimes. Mass shootings of movie goers in Aura, CO and Sandy Hook elementary school were horrible tragedies that rightly deserved much media attention. But because they deserved large amounts of media attention does not mean they are the typical or the most frequently occurring type of gun crime and while many people died in each incident, it does not mean that the majority of gun deaths happen in this particular type of gun crime, mass shootings. The great media attention distorts our perspective somewhat from the reality of each situation. While Aura and Sandy Hook were terrible tragedies, they were still relatively rare occurrences. They should never have happened, but they are rare occurrences. Many crime statistics report that mass shootings are actually declining in the United States. The victims in each were killed by uniquely motivated individuals, individuals that would most likely have used other means of destruction if firearms were made unavailable to them. Aura and Sandy Hook were not accidental deaths from a robbery gone wrong or a gang motivated shooting, they were planned and perpetrated by individuals with abnormal motivations and goals.

And while Aura and Sandy Hook, in the grand scheme of gun crimes, were rare events, every single day children and young adults are being killed by illegally obtained guns in America's inner cities. Why are we not as outraged by this daily occurrence of death in our inner cities? Perhaps we have become acculturated to it, that we are no longer shocked into action. The vast majority of shootings in our inner cities involve illegally obtained guns. The average mafia member, gangbanger, or cartel member could not pass many background checks required for legal purchase of firearms. Therefore a national solution must focus on and address illegally obtained firearms as well as unregulated loopholes such as gun shows and outdated laws in order to curtail the gun violence that is killing people every single day in America's inner cities. Focusing on limiting access to guns by those who seek guns through illegal channels will not prevent criminals from obtaining guns.

---

[19] Illegally obtained – referring to guns obtained through secondary markets: gun shows, pawn shops, unlicensed dealers, personal sales, thefts, etc.

Given that the vast majority of gun crimes involve illegally obtained firearms, I believe a politically viable solution for both major parties exists that will also tackle the largest portion of gun crimes in the United States. Those on the left that advocate for a gun control policy which incorporates greater limits on access to firearms obtained legally, should have very little, if any, opposition to legislation tackling illegal firearms. Those on the right who advocate gun owner rights for legal gun owners should provide very little if any opposition as well. By removing illegal guns which account for over 80% of gun crimes, the United States is decreasing the overall destruction and loss of life caused by guns, which is the stated goal of enacting gun control legislation of those on the left. By removing illegal guns, the United States is being tough on crime by depriving criminals of the most common weapon of deadly force and decreasing gun crimes which paint all guns, including legal guns, in a highly negative light, the aim of contemporary conservative agendas. Any compromise between the left and right political factions in the United States will have to center on a common ground, built by small concessions on each side. Those on the left will have to abandon their desire for removing legal guns from society. If a person is a law abiding citizen, who can pass a background check, they should have the right to own gun.[20] The left will have to grant the rights of law abiding citizens who can pass a background check to own guns. Those on the right will have to accept limitations on illegally purchased guns and gun loopholes, aimed at individuals ability to purchase firearms illegally, not legal firearm purchases. To achieve the aim of placing limitations on illegal firearm purchases, the right will have to accept laws limiting the behavior and access to illegal firearms and greater regulation of firearm dealers including gun shows. Admittedly, given the current political climate this may be difficult to say the least. The right has showed an extreme unwillingness to compromise on any aspect of gun control, even gun control focused on illegal firearms. The tradeoff between left and right will be thus; the right accepts greater regulation and requirements on the gun industry in exchange for protections of legal gun owners, the undeniable right of law abiding citizens to own firearms. Under this agreement, the right acquiesces to gun regulation focused on illegally obtained firearms in exchange for the left agreeing to draw the line with illegally obtained firearms, the right wins the right to own firearms, which is what they claim is the reason they are fighting the left tooth and nail. Also, focusing on illegal firearms aligns with the rights desire to be 'tough' on crime and eliminates the gun crime. I believe illegal guns to be the most likely avenue, within the current gun debate, the right may be willing to regulate. Under this agreement, the left is allowed to pass legislation limiting illegally obtained guns, the guns involved in over 80% of gun crimes, saving thousands of lives annually, the left's stated reason for pursuing gun control. I believe this basic compact will be necessary to move forward. Focusing on illegal guns is not only the most effective way to decrease gun violence in the United States, but also the most politically feasible as well.

---

[20] Guns are a force equalizer. The physical attributes of the user are relegated to secondary importance one they are wielding a gun. There are several safety and societal implications of the force equalizing capacity of guns. One being, they do allow for women to achieve parity with men, where without a gun, a women is at a distinct physical disadvantage against a man wishing to do her harm.

Within the guise of regulating the gun industry, there are a few specific areas of concern I would like to call attention to and elaborate on; gun shows, unlicensed dealers, and loopholes in gun selling laws. First, proper regulation of gun shows should be of paramount priority, specifically the regulation of unlicensed gun dealers who sell weapons at these shows. Gun shows are ill regulated and provide an easy route for those wishing to purchase guns outside of the legal system. Guns obtained illegally at gun shows also provided the bulk of firearms used by Mexican drug cartels in Mexico, which means that illegal American guns were used in the killing of tens of thousands of Mexicans during the drug wars between Mexican drug cartels. Gun shows either need to be properly monitored and regulated or shut down entirely. Proper regulation of gun shows and the unlicensed venders who find a home in gun shows will greatly reduce the flow illegal guns into the hands of criminals.

Many states have loopholes in their gun laws that allow for guns to be sold to individuals who under normal circumstances would not be able to purchase guns. For example many states have a loophole that specifies that if a gun store is going out of business they may sell guns to whoever they wish regardless of existing laws. We need to close these loopholes. In a similar fashion we need to enact serious penalties for breaking these new laws and engaging in the unlicensed and unregulated sale of firearms. Ultimately the United States needs to create a properly regulated market for the buying and selling of guns. A market where responsible law abiding citizens have the ability to purchase guns and criminals are prevented from obtaining guns and their deadly potential should be the general goal of those overseeing a regulated market. In order to achieve a properly functioning regulated market the US must make gun sales by unlicensed dealers illegal and crack down on those dealers that persist. Authorities should also crack down on the sale of guns by pawn shops and other secondary markets.

Another option could be the creation of a national or statewide gun registry. We currently require and have a registry for cars, why not one for guns. Vehicular deaths far outpace gun deaths annually in the United States. We also require citizens to obtain basic credentials for operating a motor vehicle, a driver's license; so that other drivers know each person has passed certain criteria for safe driving. Perhaps one needs a license to operate a gun. A basic set of guidelines that need to be met, proper usage procedures and safe storage information perhaps could be obtained in order to operate a gun. It would not illegal to own a gun, but to properly utilize one without a license. We have licenses for cars and they do not infringe on the rights of individuals to own weapons, neither does a registry. We restrict criminals from voting, so there is a president for the suspension of certain civil rights. We also keep track of criminals after they have been paroled, when they have supposedly paid their debt to society. What this last point is getting at is that there is a precedent for placing restrictions on the rights of some individuals. So placing restrictions on criminals from obtaining guns has a precedent.

In my opinion, most of the debate around gun control in the United States is a false debate. Those advocating on each side of the debate are motivated more by ideology and ideological purity than finding a pragmatic solution to save the lives of Americans who are killed every year by gun violence. A pragmatic solution that works to deprive criminals of guns by shutting down secondary markets is the most effective solution. By going after illegally obtained guns, the United States will be going after guns involved in over 80% of gun crimes. The pragmatic central elements of each of the two main political parties can find a politically acceptable solution to the gun debate in the United States. By focusing more on a pragmatic solution that address the real core issues of the gun debate, the United States can create a safer country that also respects the individual rights of gun owners.

Tax Structure

In the future the United States will be constrained financially with paying down its considerable debt and paying increasing medical costs for retiring baby boomers. In this new world of financial constraint, it will be important for the United States to be as efficient as possible with its resources. Efficiency will be more important than quantity. From my analysis, and I am not alone, the United States tax code leaves much to be desired. In addition to being the longest document in human history, the United States tax code is very inefficient at utilizing the resources of the United States. The current United States tax code and larger tax system is horribly inefficient for raising revenue, contributes to the lobbying phenomena of elected public servants, hinders the efficient allocation of capital, and is disadvantageous to those without a financial education and those who can afford financial counseling. I believe to assuage these problems, the United States should move towards a tax system that utilizes a flat tax, both for income and corporate income. The United States should also adopt a federal sales tax to be applied on top of state sales taxes as well. The adoption of a combination flat tax and national sales tax will put the United States on found financial footing, will represent the most significant effort to contain lobbying in the modern era, make the tax system more accessible to citizens by reducing the financial education bias, and helps facilitate efficient allocation of capital.

From an economic perspective, tax breaks to the extent that they are currently employed by the United States hurt the efficient allocation of capital in the US on a corporate and individual level. If tax breaks influence the operations of a business or how a business spends its revenues, this creates a distortion. A business should be making decisions based primarily on what is best for their business operations, not by saving money through certain tax loopholes. If a business makes a decision on production methods based on a desired tax loophole and not on what is best for their overall operational efficiency, this business is making decisions counter to its nature. These perverse incentives can lead businesses to invest too much or too little, to shift production to certain areas, and/or issue unneeded debt[21] all in the name of saving money from taxes. These loopholes and tax breaks distort the normal business operations and allocation of capital.

On a personal income level, tax breaks can cause altered savings rates, consumption habits, and many other aspects as individuals choose to allocate their resources to more tax friendly areas and instruments. From an economic perspective, these tax breaks create distortions in the normal flow of the market and affect the efficient allocation of capital by artificially pushing capital into other areas. A flat corporate and personal income tax would eliminate these distortions and force people to make decisions less because of tax reasons and more on normal economic rational.

---

[21] As Apple recently did with their debt offering.

It is important to note that a tax break is, in absolute terms, equivalent to a subsidy payment for the amount of the tax break. Either way, the firm or person has the amount of money specified and the government does not. This has produced and fuelled lobbing efforts by wealthy individuals, corporations, and unions, amongst many others, to take advantage of our current malleable tax code. These individuals and entities invest very heavily in lobbying firms and PACs in order to curry favor with elected officials. A possible by product of excessive lobbying efforts could be the end result of elected public servants making decisions based more on large campaign contributions then than the needs of their constituents. This creates a distortion in democracy in the US and contributes to the dysfunction within the government. By removing these tax breaks (subsidies) from the US tax code, one removes financial incentives for lobbying and we can go a long way to reducing the influence of lobbyists, corporations, and wealthy individuals on our elected officials and the democratic process. Also, a flat tax would eliminate any government favoritism for certain firms or industries through tax breaks. Since there would be very few tax breaks, it would remove a vehicle from which corporations influence elected officials and decrease their power over the electoral process by eliminating their financial incentive to influence officials and the electoral process.

The tax code is littered with exceptions and conditions which are very difficult for the average person to interpret, much less understand to a degree to take advantage of them. The United States tax code is the longest document in human history. It is over 17,000 pages long. It is huge and incredibly difficult to navigate sufficiently. The size and complexity of the US tax code severs to disenfranchise those who are not financial sophisticated (through financial education or family knowledge) and those who cannot afford the services of a tax and/or finance professional. Much is said about the unfairness of the tax code, favoring the wealthy, recently this criticism has come due to historically low top marginal rate that the highest income earners in the United States pay. But the unfairness of the complexity of the tax code, which favors the wealthy, is not discussed as often or with the same amount of candor and seriousness. Many wealthy citizens of the US have sophisticated knowledge of finance and the US tax code, which allows them to minimize their tax payments. Or if a person is sufficiently wealthy they may hire a person with sophisticated finance and tax knowledge to help them take advantage of the tax code. The uneducated, the reasonably educated, and the poor are at an inherit disadvantage with the current tax code. Creating a flat tax for personal income would eliminate tax breaks and make the tax code much more manageable. A few tax breaks could be kept, but the US could surly shrink the tax code down to a 12 to 15 page document, a length any high school graduate could navigate. Without multiple tax breaks, a person could simply apply their income amount to the flat tax percentage and easily calculate their tax payment, again something any high school graduate could perform.

The US has the second highest corporate tax rate in the industrialized world. When factoring in state corporate income tax rates on top of the national sales tax rate, the US has the highest corporate tax rates in the industrialized world. Due to tax breaks in the current US tax code, there is much variety on what rate US corporations actually or effectively pay.[22] No matter one's political persuasions, it does not seem likely the US can be competitive in the world with US companies carrying such a high tax burden. In the era of globalization with its ease of capital and human flows across borders, it is imperative that the US become an attractive place for companies to do business in all aspects, especially in regards to tax policy. The US needs to be an attractive place for companies in order to retain the companies and their operations that are currently in the US but also to attract new companies operating outside the US to the US and to encourage new companies to be founded in the US. A flat corporate tax would eliminate almost every tax break currently offered to US firms. This would intern raise revenue the federal government collects. The US could then in turn drastically lower the corporate tax rate to accommodate the new raise in revenues collected. Given that current federal revenues from corporate income taxes amount to approximately 8% of total federal revenues, any fluctuation in revenue collected from the new flat tax corporate structure would have a very minimal impact on the federal budget. Also on that same line of thinking, a 2% or 3% drop in revenue, as a percentage of the entire federal revenue total, from corporate taxes would be relative insignificant when compared to the benefits from creating a more competitive and encouraging business environment within the United States. Perhaps the better and more competitive business environment within the US, as a result of lowered corporate tax rates, might spur greater business growth and thus higher tax revenues as a result of growing the amount of business done in the US or more colloquially, growing the size of the business pie instead of the percentage of the total of the slice. Simply, creating a more business friendly environment should take precedence over any lost corporate tax revenue because the loss of revenue will undoubtedly be very minimal in regards to the overall US federal revenues.

Due to states having corporate income taxes as well, if a reduction in the federal corporate income tax was to be implemented, thought must be given to state tax rates as well. A state in a less than desirable fiscal situation[23], might find it favorable to increase its corporate tax in conjunction with a lowered federal tax in order to raise more revenue for the state. A state could justify this by raising their rate less than the drop in the federal rate, therefore proclaiming that the corporation is still better off than they were before. This practice must be curtailed or the point of dropping the federal corporate tax rate will be for not. Therefore a cap on state corporate income tax should somehow be imposed on states by the federal government. This can be achieved either by creating a hard cap percentage number or by limiting state corporate income tax rates to a certain proportion of the federal. The currently average US state corporate income tax rate is approximately 7.5%. It would be suggested that the federal government cap the state rate around 7.5%. If the federal government were to lower the corporate tax rate to 10%, a proportionate cap of ¾ of the federal level could be imposed for states as an example.

---

[22] For example, in recent years Goldman Sachs paid a 33% tax rate while General Electric paid 0.5%.
[23] Such as California or Illinois to name just two of many.

With a flat tax for personal income, a person who has a higher income would pay more in taxes than someone with a lower income, their payment would just be proportional to their income. Many people would find this a more 'fair' tax policy, that everyone should pay the same proportion of their income and that a graduated income system penalized those who are successful. This is admittedly a subjective argument, but one that will most likely resonate with many Americans. A flat tax for personal income may also serve as a logical relief to the wealthy who have lost their educational and wealth advantage from the old (current US) tax code.

A Federal sales tax is very similar to a value-added tax. A sales tax is a much more feasible option in the US because of the prevailing political climate in the US. Given a large section of the US's population aversion to anything considered to be even remotely related to socialism or government control it would be very difficult to get a value-added tax passed. Many would see a value-added tax as creeping European socialism, since it is most commonly seen in widespread use in Europe. However irrational this argument may be, it would carry much weight and prevent the adoption of a value-added tax in the United States. Simply put, a value-added tax is unfamiliar to the American public and thus would face opposition, also due to its unfamiliarity, it would be considered foreign by many Americans. A sales tax is a concept and terminology that is already in use in the US through state sales taxes. This familiarity with and acceptance of the state sales tax would make the adoption of a national sales tax much easier. It is much easier to argue for something on the national level that is already in place on the state level.

A national sales tax would further benefit those who save and consume less. After the 2007 financial crisis, much was made of the negative attributes of Americans' over consumption and incredibly low historical savings rates.[24] By imposing a national sales tax on non-essential items, those who choose to spend more will pay more in taxes. Those who utilize their income for mostly essential means such as food, transport, education, and other essentials (what most of the poor spend their limited means on) will pay less in taxes. Those who over indulge on huge televisions, yachts, and luxury cars will pay more in taxes. Those who save will pay less. A national sales tax also means that the wealthy will pay more in taxes than the poor. A 5% sales tax on a 100,000 dollar Mercedes is much more than a 5% sales tax on a 15,000 dollar Honda, a 5000 dollar to 750 dollar comparison. As well, when the federal government derives revenue from a federal sales tax, they will be able to lower the flat tax rate to compensate. This will further benefit those who save, since the flat tax rate is reduced and they pay less in income taxes because of the federal sales tax.

Ultimately one must assign percentages to the various new tax rates. It goes without saying that much research and intellect must be spent determining the appropriate percentages for these taxes. Due to the difficulty in adopting a new tax at a national level where one of its kind did not previously exist, it would be better to keep the national sales tax at a lower level. A

---

[24] At one point before the financial crisis the US savings rate dipped below zero, it became negative.

suggestion of 2% to 5% would be appropriate for a national sales tax. A national flat income tax rate could exist between 15% and 20%. A corporate income tax rate of 10% would be advisable with a state rate capped at ¾ of the federal rate, creating an effective upper limit of the state rate at 7.5%, the current national average. This would create a 17.5% max effective tax rate for US corporations. Given that the current US federal tax rate is 35%, before any tax deductions, (without adding in state tax rates, which would make the average tax rate 42.5% before tax deductions) 17.5% would be very favorable and go a long way to creating a more encouraging environment for business in the US.

While the adoption of a flat tax and national sales tax will certainly not solve all of the tax related problems currently confronting the United States, it will provide the United States with a simpler more efficient tax system. The combination of a flat tax and national sales tax is more efficient in raising revenues, removes major incentives for lobbying, removes a financial knowledge bias, may raise more money, and promotes economic growth over the current tax structure and system. The ideas presented in this essay are not meant as a hard and fast plan that is immediately actionable. They are meant to provoke thought and discussion on improving the current the United States tax code.

National Debt

Most conversations revolving around the United States' national debt and any plan to pay off the national debt are influenced too heavily by political considerations and do not take into effect enough economic or long-term thinking. While this is understandable, it is not productive for the United States reducing its debt burdening in an effective, responsible way. Too often conservatives boldly speak of paying down the national debt within a ten year time span, only made possible with truly draconian spending cuts, while liberals fail to give any significant attention to the United States' ballooning national debt. I will make several general proposals that will constitute the basic framework for a plan to responsibility pay off the national debt of the United States within a reasonable timeframe[25].

The United States should set a 30 to 40, possibly even 50, year timeline for paying off our national debt. By taking 30 or more years the United States will be able to pay off our national debt in regular manageable installments that still give us the financial flexibility to invest in key areas of concern; education and infrastructure for example. If we were to set a 10 year time span, the payments the United States would have to make would be very large and require truly draconian cuts to public spending that would make any investment in education and infrastructure unfeasible[26]. Liken a payment timeframe to a home mortgage an individual may take out in order to purchase a house. That individual could pay off their house, a rather large sum of money for the vast majority of American citizens, in a ten year time span, but the monthly payments would be oppressive for that individual. They would not be able to afford to pay for virtually any recreational activity, take a limited vacation, utilize furniture, or have any creature comforts. The bulk of their income would be dedicated towards making payments for their house. Comically that individual might be limited to living on inflatable furniture, eating hot dogs, and drinking tang, all that they could afford. By spreading their mortgage out to 30 years, they are able to make payments on their house and to live a more comfortable life; taking vacations, going to the cinema, attending sporting events, eating a wider range of food, and so on. By creating a 30 or 40 year plan to pay off our national debt, the United States can make the payments necessary to pay off our national debt and still have the financial flexibility to pay for spending on education and infrastructure.

Adopting a logical, credible plan to pay down our national debt is all that is needed to restore what investor confidence the United States lost in the recent political debt ceiling

---

[25] An interesting point to consider would be in a hypothetical scenario where the United States has paid off its national debt, how would the United States conduct monetary policy? Is there another market that is as deep and as liquid as the current US treasuries market? Conducting monetary policy may become a much more complicated and tricky business.

[26] Given the fiscal challenges confronting the United States currently and in the future, it seems imperative for the United States to invest its resources as efficiently as possible.

standoff. The United States was downgraded from its AAA bond rating not for any financial inability to pay off our existing debt, but because of a perceived lack of political will to pass a workable solution to pay off our debt. While I have my concerns with the rational for the downgrade; mainly that rating agencies are taking an inherently objective problem, does the United States have the ability to pay its debt obligations, and applying a subjective lens, will the United States pay its debt obligation, it is undeniable that the United States has suffered a loss of credibility in the international world. Simple enacting a credible debt reduction plan will increase the credit rating of the United States. The United States has the ability to pay off our national debt; the only question is will the United States pay off our national debt. With the passage of a credible plan, the question is answered. The United States is not Argentina, who seemingly every decade defaults on their debt obligations and forces investors to take a haircut on their bonds. Argentina is a country that is not perceived to always honor their debt obligations. The United States is one of only four countries to never miss a debt payment, along with France, Canada, and Australia. The United States is well respected in the international community and the international community has full confidence the United States will meet its debt obligations. Again, the United States is not Argentina. If we submit a plan to reduce our national debt to reasonable levels, the international community will be satisfied.

I believe a concrete, rational 30 to 40 year plan to reduce the national debt of the United States will be a responsible way for the United States to reduce its national debt that still gives the United States the financial flexibility to invest in education and infrastructure. It will restore any lost confidence in the United States from an international financial market perspective. The United States would do well to adopt a logical plan under the general framework proposed in the this essay to reduce its national debt.

Voting on Same Sex Marriage

I don't have to tell any reader about the attention surrounding the issue popularly known as gay marriage. With the Supreme Court is currently hearing the California Prop 8 challenge, every media outlet and partisan hack has been commenting, one way or another, on gay marriage and its possible ramifications for American society. Will it open the flood gates for all kinds of marriage or will it normalize the virtual relationships, identical to traditional marriages in all but name, that many Americans have long been involved? Will we finally give homosexuals the basic civil rights that they have long been denied? These are certainly important questions, but I can't help but wonder if we are overlooking the most important question of all that seems to be lost in the whole California Prop 8 spectacle, should we even be voting a person's civil rights? Should we put a person's civil rights up to a popular vote, as we have done in California with Prop 8? Should a minority's civil rights be at the mercy of popular opinion and the tyranny of the majority? The answers to these questions lie in definitively defining freedom of sexuality, and by extension gay marriage, as a civil right, and in our own, American history with civil rights. At this point, overwhelming consensus is that sexuality is a civil right.

In the United States we currently define; gender, race, religion, ethnicity, and age as civil rights and provide adequate protection against discrimination by our laws. Sexuality, specifically homosexuality in this case, isn't any different from gender, race, religion, ethnicity, or age. First, if you think that a person is born with their sexuality, for simple example, that a person is born homosexual or heterosexual, then you would think they have no control over their sexuality. A person is also born with their race, gender, and ethnicity and one has little control over one's age, so sexuality is very similar in lack of choice. On the other hand, if you happen to be of the persuasion that sexuality is a choice, for example, one chooses to be heterosexual or homosexual, then sexuality has freedom of choice in common with religion. Either way, one can view sexuality under the guise of existing civil rights.

Let's turn the table 180 degrees with an experiment. Imagine a world which exists exactly as it does today, with the notable exception that traditional sexuality, homosexual and heterosexual, norms are reversed. Homosexuals are in the majority and heterosexuals the minority. Homosexual, same sex, marriage is legal and heterosexual marriage is not. Most American opponents of same sex marriage would be outraged to live in such a world. When "The Crooked Man" by Charles Beaumont, which depicted just such a scenario, was published in Playboy in 1955 it created a stir and outrage. People were very upset and expressed their frustration in harsh language and terse words in letters to Playboy. People were clearly outraged. The lesson to be learned from this experiment is that if it was wrong to persecute heterosexuals in a homosexual majority world, it is wrong to persecute homosexuals in a heterosexual majority world. These points taken in aggregate lead me to believe that we should define sexuality as a civil right.

You may ask, how does sexuality as a civil right relate to marriage? The United States government recognizes secular marriages regardless of common civil rights; race, religion, ethnicity, and age. Sexuality should not be considered as well. In a world in which the US government doesn't define marriage by any religious definition, the government would not be bounded to defining marriage between different genders, as many religions do.

Some would argue that a marriage is based on the union of two people for procreation, but many married heterosexual couples choose not to have children. If we allow these childless couples to remain married, then marriage is based on the union of two people, not just for procreation. If procreation is no longer considered, the sexuality of partners is no longer important, and thus there is no basis to discriminate on basis of sexuality in marriage in regards to procreation. By this new definition of marriage, there is no reason why same sex partners should not enjoy the civil right of marriage. To deny same sex partners marriage based on their sexuality, would be to deny them their civil rights. Which leads back to the original question, should we be putting someone's civil rights up to a popular vote? The second part of the answer to that question lies in our past history with civil rights.

We did not put the civil rights of African-Americans in the South to a popular vote. The federal government took action. How much longer would it have taken African-Americans in Southern states to realize their civil rights if we had let voters in Southern states such as Alabama, Arkansas, Louisiana, and Mississippi vote on African-American civil rights? How much longer would it have taken us to dismantle segregation in the South if we had put it up to a popular vote in the South? We didn't put the civil rights of African-Americans to state wide popular votes in the Southern states because we didn't want African-Americans to be subject to the tyranny of the white majority. If this is the lesson we have learned from our history with African-American civil rights, then why are we not following it now? If we knew it was wrong to put the civil rights of African-Americans to a popular vote, why are we putting the civil rights of homosexuals to a popular vote, to be at the whims of popular sentiment? Why would we put the civil rights of homosexuals at the mercy of the tyranny of the majority?

"The right of every American to first-class citizenship is the most important issue of our time," Jackie Robinson. Ultimately, it is a travesty that in 2013 the words of Jackie Robinson still ring true. We have a group of fellow Americans that cannot realize their civil rights and who effectively have second class citizenship. As worse, we are putting their civil rights to a popular vote, just like any other ballet initiative. No one's civil rights should be put at the mercy and whims of a popular opinion. No one's civil rights should be under the tyranny of the majority. Good thing for Jackie Robinson that the decision to allow him to play baseball wasn't put up to a popular vote. Hopefully the Supreme Court will render this point moot and we can finally realize Jackie Robinson's dream of an America where every citizen enjoys first-class citizenship.

Addendum thought passage: Cause of Traditional Religious Communities to Same Sex Marriage

I think the root of religious opposition, and most opposition for that matter, to same sex marriage has to do with power dynamics. Religious communities are losing power in United States culture and same sex marriage is a graphic representation of the struggle they are losing. As the power of religious communities continues to decrease in the United States, their opposition will only grow more vocal and severe.

While not discussed often, there is tremendous power in the ability to define a society's ethics and morals. The general ethics and morals of a society provide the internal mental controls that govern much of the behavior of individuals. They inform what kind of behavior and, more importantly, thoughts are deemed acceptable and actionable. Throughout the majority of human history, religious thinking has carried enormous sway over every day human behavior, most often setting the laws of a nation state. Only relatively recently have secular forces been able to define laws, but religious forces still hold great influence over society. Very recently, in the western world, religious forces have been losing their influence and control over society as well. Much has been made in the press about a post Christian Europe and increasingly an irrelevance of religion in the United States. Any number of cultural battles in society have been won by secular forces. Compared to 50 years ago, religious communities have much less influence and control over society today. I think this loss of power to influence the ethics and morals of society is the main driving factor behind the intense opposition to same sex marriage in the United States.

Same sex marriage is seen as a defining representation of this power battle by religious communities in the United States. Religious communities need to recognize that the power paradigm is shifting. They have lost much influence among the young and this will cause them to have decreasing power as their older adherents die without younger cohorts to replace them. They have already lost power on this issue. Better to embrace gay marriage and shepherd it into their existing morals and to preserve what power they do have.

When in history have those in power willingly let go of power? There are very few examples throughout history, if any, when a particular group has ceded power without compensation. I do not believe that current religious communities in the United States will cede their remaining cultural power easily. We should expect opposition to continue.

Justification for Some Degree of a Socialist State

Often I have encountered individuals who hold very firm and passionate philosophical views on the nature of political systems. Rarely, upon further questioning, have I found the majority of individuals to possess the ability to explain why they hold these passionate philosophical views on the nature of political systems. Simply put, many feel very strongly about the importance of their political philosophy without being able to explain why. One could hold a very strong belief in the importance of government welfare programs without being able to justify having government programs as a concept. Upon rumination, I wondered if perhaps I could explain my own views. The essay that follows is a running serious of thoughts designed at examining a society, individuals within that society, and the role of a government in a society and any responsibilities to the individual a government may have. Again this essay is a though exercise and not a definite view of society or an expression of my views. At the end of the though experiment in this essay, I came to see the need for government programs as well as free market competition. Both vital and both need the other.

In general, a person cannot control who their parents are or where they are born as they are not born and unable to influence decisions. If one holds a deterministic view of the world, perhaps influenced by particle physics theory, then they arrive at the conclusion that theoretically we do not have free will, and thus no control over the circumstances we are born into. As well, a person exerts very little control over the environment they are raised in, one is almost most entirely at the mercy of exogenous forces well beyond their control. All of these previous points taken together create seemingly random or predetermined circumstances into which individuals are born. Any objective observer of humanity in any country and society on earth which humans inhabit, can reach a conclusion that people are born into different circumstances. The seemingly arbitrary or predetermined disparity in the circumstances one is born into has been a vexing concern of humans for our entire history. For the largest portion of human history the circumstances one was born into dictated the outcome of their life, from their occupation to their life expectancy to who they would marry. The crushing reality of the predetermined circumstances of life must have been before in history, as it is now, extremely difficult to handle without an outlet to alleviate the pressure or a suitable explanation for the preordained circumstances of life. Into this vacuum stepped religion, especially the religious concept of an afterlife. The religious concept of an afterlife was the key to being able to cope with and find meaning in the seemingly random and arbitrary circumstances an individual may have found themselves born. If the life being lived currently on earth was but a mere prelude to an infinitely longer and just afterlife, then the experiences, trials, and tribulations being experienced on earth would be bearable, even justified. One's trails and hardships could be a test by God to see if one was worthy or the next life. Religion in many ways could be viewed, in part, as a way of intellectually rationalizing and justifying the human condition and the seemingly random disparities in living conditions in human society. Religion and the concept of an afterlife made much of human existence bearable. Religion was a way to explain the arbitrary circumstances into which individuals were born. After the enlightenment and increased moves towards secular culture and society, the religious concept of heaven no longer held the same power to alleviate the disparity in living conditions, which were still primarily determined by the socio-economic conditions one was born into, humans experienced in society. A new justification for the arbitrary disparity in socio-economic birth circumstances or ability to alleviate pressure caused by this disparity needed to emerge for people in society. In the void left by religion stepped economics and government.

John Stuart Mill, Alfred Marshall, Karl Marx, John Maynard Keyes, and many more economists were primarily concerned with alleviating the deplorable economic conditions '9/10s' of human beings were born into and formed the cages which caused them to become trapped. Whether through productivity gains, curing the business cycle, or other means, each tried to find ways produced by humans to ameliorate the arbitrariness of the socio-economic conditions into which one was born. I think the most important take away from the previous paragraphs is that in a world where God does not exist or there is no way to prove of an afterlife with the promise of redemption in it, human beings must take action to ameliorate the randomness[27] and disparity of the conditions in a society into which individuals are born and live. Without any guarantee of an afterlife, the one life individuals are born into is of paramount importance. Based on a Judeo-Christian view of fairness that dominates secular western society, if individuals would like to make a fair society for all, that society must take it upon themselves to alleviate a degree of the randomness of circumstances of individuals' birth. Again, in a world without God, individuals must create a solution to make society fairer.

What actions a society must take to produce a society where individuals are not trapped by the socio-economic circumstance into which they are born is a highly debated issue. The collective representation of society is generally a government, hopefully a representative democracy. As individuals we come together with other individuals and sacrifice some personal freedoms for the benefits of a society that we could not obtain on our own but only with the combined efforts with others; hospitals and healthcare, avenues for trade that allow individuals to spend their time on other pursuits than growing or hunting our own food, schools, a police force protect citizens, a monetary system, a military to provide us with protection from outside threats, and so on. The most common enabler and dispenser of these collective societal goods such as school systems and police forces is a government. It would stand to reason that the best avenue then for mitigating the arbitrary nature of socio-economic circumstances inherited at birth would be a government, considering that a government already has most of the societal tools to mitigate

---

[27] Randomness in this context is 'relative randomness' or 'seemingly random.' In a theoretical deterministic worldview, nothing is random. Due to practical limitations of the human mind, events seem random, so therefore for practical purposes they are random, although theoretically they are not.

circumstances of birth. It would seem that a socialist state is the best method for taking action to create a fairer society.[28]

It is important to note that virtually all of people living in the world today already accept a socialistic society, only differing in degrees of socialism. If a person has no moral qualms with sending their children to a public school, that is a school funded primarily by taxes, they have accepted a socialist program and by extension a socialistic state. It would be very difficult to argue against a socialistic state in the absolute sense, but plausible to argue against the degree of a socialistic state. As a result of this thinking, extending government programs to combat the arbitrary nature of birth socio-economic condition is merely an extension of the existing type of government. Furthermore one could argue that socialistic programs already exist in the form of tax payer funded public schools, which are also meant to alleviate the disparity in parents ability to provide schooling for their children which is of course a socio-economic condition determined at birth. Without public school, society would be left in a medieval state where only the wealthy can afford tutors for their children, who will be the only children to receive an education.

What the previous paragraphs are getting at is the need for government programs to combat the seemingly random nature and disparity in the socio-economic circumstances inherited at birth. A socialist state with government programs is then a way of alleviating the seeming randomness and disparity in society originating from birth circumstances.[29] Given that in a world without God or a guarantee of an afterlife where the world an individual is born into is all they may be able to live, it is imperative that that individual not be trapped by the socio-economic circumstances of their birth.

It is important to recognize that by entering into a society we accept limitations on individuality and individual power. These limitations cause much friction in the world as individuals confront these limitations to their own power. An expansion of the socialistic state will only cause more limitations on individual power and create more frictions between the individual and society. I do not think this process can be avoided. A very real danger is that too many restrictions on individual power many inhibit the ability of the individual to reach their full potential, which most can agree is counterproductive to the goal socialistic government programs were first trying to conquer. From the previous sentences, the operative question thus presented is as follows, is the collective potential of those raised by the socialist state to levels they could not have achieved in the circumstances they are born into greater than the loss of potential from increased societal restrictions to individuals? I believe the aforementioned question to be of paramount importance when constructing socialistic government programs intended to

---

[28] Justification of socialism may depend on God. Perhaps this assertion paints Jesus and his message in a new light. Perhaps Jesus was advocating for helping the poor in a way to ameliorate the randomness of the world.
[29] From the ideas postulated above, the neo-conservative movement needs religion to justify their social and economic policies. The prospect of an eternal reward or destination is central to allowing for a lack of social programs. If God doesn't exist, then their politics become much more difficult to defend. God is a built in safety net for them, a built in social safety net.

ameliorate disparity in the socio-economic circumstances into which individuals are born. We do not want to raise individuals from their socio-economic circumstances only to crush their individual potential by societal restrictions.[30] So then how do we maximize the amelioration of random circumstances born into and minimize society inhibiting the greatness of individuals in the construction of the socialist state?

In regards to the question posed above, expanding the socialistic state to its logical conclusion, which would be communism, does not satisfy both conditions of the posed in the question. While a pure communistic state would eradicate any variance in socio-economic circumstances at birth, it would come at the cost of inhibiting the potential of individuals. In such a regimented and structured society, more societal and government restrictions on personal behavior and exercise of personal power are an inevitable consequence of government efforts to eradicate any disparity in socio-economic circumstances inherited from birth. In order to ensure no individual gains an advantage from their birth socio-economic circumstances a government would have to provide each individual with the same of virtually everything; the same education, the same food intake, same living accommodations, same healthcare opportunities, and so on. A strictly pure communistic state would eradicate the disparity in inherited birth socio-economic circumstances, but would come at too high a cost in limiting personal freedom and potential. This line of thinking is not condemning communism as an evil ideology, just as an ideology not suited to providing a solution to the current question posed. If one wishes only to eliminate the disparity in birth socio-economic circumstances in society, communism will accomplish that goal, but not maximizing human potential. So, socialistic government policies alone cannot solve the dilemma posed. I think the solution to this problem involves the pairing of socialistic government programs with capitalistic competition, specifically regulated market competition.

I imagine the pairing in general working as follows; utilizing government policies enough to allow every citizen access to the field of play and once on the field of play, competition determines the success of an individual. If disparities in socio-economic conditions arise, they may primarily arise from disparities in performance against competition on the field of play. Government programs do not need to ensure that every individual arrives on the field with the same abilities and circumstances, there will be disparities in abilities of those who enter the field as in basketball with those of different heights and muscle masses, but government programs need to make sure every individual has access to the field of play. Using basketball for a further example, Chris Paul is of below average height for the NBA, but he has been extraordinarily successful despite his smaller than average height, what was most important was that he was given the opportunity to prove himself. I think government programs should be utilized to ameliorate disparities in birth socio-economic circumstances to the point that they

---

[30] All of these justifications mentioned could be used to justify general tolerance and classic libertarianism. As long as one is not impeding the livelihood of someone else or hurting anyone, once can be left to do what one wants to do. The circumstances we are born into are arbitrary and out of our control, so putting limitations on them is just as arbitrary, unless they impede someone's ability to live their life.

allow everyone to participate in the economy and society[31], no more than is needed to give every individual access. At the end of the reach of government programs is where regulated free market competition will pick up.

In a deterministic world being considered in this essay, individuals do not have any control over the socio-economic circumstances into which they are born. Capitalistic competition offers the ability to take control over the course of one's life, but this can only happen if one is not trapped by the socio-economic circumstances of their birth. Government programs allow those to gain access to the field, but it is up to the individual to play well. Capitalistic competition allows an individual to improve the socio-economic circumstances of their life, which they were prevented from having any control over at birth. In a society and market based system that is based on ability and competition, one's present abilities matter more than the circumstances of one's birth. The circumstances may give one an advantage in abilities, but they are not the final say, personal responsibility is the final say, it places most of the responsibility on the individual to do the best with their resources. The job of social programs is to provide every person, regardless of birth circumstances, with the minimum level to compete.

So based on what has been written above, the keys to a fair society are both socialists programs and free market competition. Socialist programs give everyone regardless of the circumstances they were born into the ability to compete with each other and with capitalistic competition, gives them a degree of control over their destiny. Socialist programs create the playing field that is used to compete freely, but market competition is just as important, it gives people control over their outcome. The only question is the degree of social programs. I think they should provide the minimum needed for people to join the conversation or game.

---

[31] I am aware of the vague and non-specific nature of this assertion. Any policy debate of any seriousness will hinge on the appropriate level of government programs. As with the rest of this essay, that assertion is meant to be considered in the realm of abstract thought.

Fernando Giannotti is a writer and economist from Dayton, Ohio. He is a member of the comedy troupe '5 Barely Employable Guys.' He holds a B.A. in economics and history and an M.S. in finance from Vanderbilt University. A self-labeled doctor of cryptozoology, he continues to live the gonzo-transcendentalist lifestyle and strives to live an examined life.

www.ingramcontent.com/pod-product-compliance
Lightning Source LLC
Chambersburg PA
CBHW060635280326
41933CB00012B/2052